the

FORTUNE TELLING

DIRECTORY

Divination Techniques to Unlock

YOUR FORTUNE

the
FORTUNE
TELLING
DIRECTORY

Divination Techniques to Unlock
YOUR FORTUNE

Isabella Drayson

chartwell
books

Brimming with creative inspiration, how-to projects, and useful information to enrich your everyday life, Quarto Knows is a favorite destination for those pursuing their interests and passions. Visit our site and dig deeper with our books into your area of interest: Quarto Creates, Quarto Cooks, Quarto Homes, Quarto Lives, Quarto Drives, Quarto Explores, Quarto Gifts, or Quarto Kids.

This edition published in 2021 by Chartwell Books,
an imprint of The Quarto Group
142 West 36th Street, 4th Floor
New York, NY 10018 USA
T (212) 779-4972 F (212) 779-6058
www.QuartoKnows.com

Originally published in 2014 as *The Secret Language of Fortune Telling.*

Chartwell titles are also available at discount for retail, wholesale, promotional, and bulk purchase. For details, contact the Special Sales Manager by email at specialsales@quarto.com or by mail at The Quarto Group, Attn: Special Sales Manager, 100 Cummings Center Suite 265D, Beverly, MA 01915 USA

10 9 8 7 6 5 4 3

ISBN: 978-0-7858-3941-5

Library of Congress Control Number: 2020952768

Conceived, designed, and produced by
The Bright Press, an imprint of The Quarto Group.
The Old Brewery, 6 Blundell Street,
London N7 9BH, United Kingdom.
T (0)20 7700 6700
www.QuartoKnows.com

Design and illustrations by Ali Walper; Cover design by Emily Nazer

Printed in China

This book provides general information. It should not be relied upon as recommending or promoting any specific diagnosis or method of treatment for a particular condition, and it is not intended as a substitute for medical advice or for direct diagnosis and treatment of a medical condition by a qualified physician. Readers who have questions about a particular condition, possible treatments for that condition, or possible reactions from the condition or its treatment should consult a physician or other.

CONTENTS

INTRODUCTION

*T*he ancient sages were fascinated by the patterns in nature. They believed these were signs sent by the gods. They noticed things like the ripples in water, the flight of birds, the lines on a tortoise's shell, or the way leaves fell on the ground. All these patterns spoke a secret language to them, revealing the truth of the past, present, and future. For thousands of years we have wanted to know about our future, and from this symbolic imagery, fortune-telling methods were developed to reveal it to us. This book takes the mystery out of the secret imagery used in fortune telling, and shows you how to read those symbols. With practical and simple step-by-step instructions, you'll discover how to interpret this secret language to create a happy and positive future for yourself and others.

This book explains all the principal and most popular forms of fortune telling and divination that are currently used. It sets out why the language of fortune telling is both literal and unique. Using the language of symbols, you will soon be able to understand not only what your individual needs are, but also how to direct your own future. This is not a science that can be measured and put into a box, but an art that adapts to each person. The aim of fortune telling is to acquire information about your current situation, to know yourself better and, of course, to plot your future. It also means that you will develop your own intuitive skills to "communicate" with the hidden forces of the cosmos.

Most people look to the future. They want to know what "will be" and how to deal with it. But knowing something about yourself in the present and past can help you to deal with that future too. You may already have experienced a feeling when you "know" or sense something is about to happen; like when someone is about to call you on the phone and then they do. This means you are unconsciously connecting with the cosmic mind deep within yourself. Using fortune telling and divination techniques gives you instant access to that pathway. This can help you make decisions and clarify your goals. It also enables you to predict the outcome of any current issue or question.

Divination and fortune telling is a way to understand and accept all the possibilities within yourself, and with that knowledge, benefit your own destiny. Your character is your fate, so enjoy discovering how to create your own good fortune.

FORTUNE TELLING

HISTORY AND LANGUAGE

*Fortune telling is based on the ancient art of divination, which was a way of reading the future through patterns, shapes, and signs in nature. The word "divination" is rooted in a Latin word, **divinare**, which means "to be inspired by a god." Throughout history, people have "divined" the future for personal or political reasons, or just to know when it was a good time to harvest the crops. Many diviners believed that their gods sent them messages and signs via the natural world. Native American Indians observed the movement of snakes; others drew pebbles from a heap. In medieval Europe, the patterns in smoke, mirrors, and fountains were divined. The Chinese and other ancient Eastern cultures threw sticks and developed intricate systems of divination based on the landscape, stars, and dragon pathways (tracks and ley lines across the countryside believed to have been created by mythical dragons).*

Fortune Fact

The Roman goddess Fortuna was the personification of luck. She was worshipped under various titles, including Fortuna Annonaria to promote a good harvest, and Fortuna Virilis to enhance a man's status or career. But not all her titles were positive. She could also be Fortuna Dubia (doubtful), Fortuna Mala (bad luck), or Fortuna Brevis (fickle).

Best of Luck

The word "fortune" comes from the Latin word *"fortuna,"* meaning luck. But of course this can mean good luck as well as bad luck. Human nature being what it is, we all want good luck and good fortune. This book guides you to develop your ability to make conscious choices based on what is good for your own life journey, and to turn negative worries or "bad luck" into good fortune.

In ancient Greece, "oracles" were priests or priestesses who acted as conduits for the gods themselves, while seers would interpret ripples on water, or markings in rocks, as signs left by the gods. The casting of bones and wooden sticks, and peering at animal entrails have all been used by ancient civilizations to predict the future. The use of dice as a fortune-telling tool is mentioned in both the Bible and the sacred Vedic script, the Rig-Veda.

During the nineteenth century, with renewed interest in spiritualism, astrology, and palmistry, fortune telling became a popular form of entertainment both at home and on the stage. With many mediums exposed as frauds, the art of fortune telling also fell into disrepute. However, divination in its occult form continued to be central to elite esoteric societies, such as the Order of the Golden Dawn. In the past twenty years or so, fortune telling has become popular again. It is a fun, fulfilling way to take control of your own destiny, and to help others do the same.

THE LANGUAGE OF SYMBOLS AND SIGNS

Most fortune-telling tools, such as the ones found in this book, are rich in symbols. The word "symbol" is from an ancient Greek word meaning "throwing together," and in a sense that's exactly what you're doing when looking at a symbol: You're being thrown together with an idea, concept, or archetypal energy that allows you to access the universal force that tells you of the past, present, and future.

A symbol always "points beyond itself" to something that is mysterious. The unique nature of the symbol is that it gives access to deeper layers of reality that are otherwise inaccessible. We all have a basic understanding of the simplest symbols. A wavy line can make us think of the sea; a jagged line of either lightning or electricity; a rose of romance; and a circle of the sun. The renowned Swiss psychologist Carl Jung proposed an alternative definition of the word "symbol" to distinguish it from a sign. In Jung's view, a sign stands for something known, while a symbol represents something that is unknown and that cannot be made clear. For example, written languages are composed of a variety of different symbols that create words. Through written words, we communicate with each other.

For thousands of years, mankind used the stars to navigate. The ancients also tried to predict the weather from patterns in the sky. They noticed how different colors of sunset and sunrise could usually imply a change in the following day's weather. They began to categorize the patterns, noticing how rain fell at certain times of year and not others. A wise man or farmer who possessed good pattern-recognition skills could predict weather outcomes to help protect his family, tribe, or country. Weather folklore was considered to be the same as fortune telling, as it also is simply about reading symbols, signs, and patterns to determine an outcome.

Fortune Fact

Edgar Cayce (1877–1944), known as the Sleeping Prophet, often spoke of the Akashic Library, a universal or divine source of meaning, where a recording from every instant that has and hasn't yet happened in time is stored. He credited it with giving him access to the past, present, and future. In a way, the symbolic language in this book is the key to opening the door of the Akashic Library.

Semiotics

Semiotics is the study of signs and symbols in communicative behavior. Semiotics focuses on the relationship of the signifier and the signified, as well as the interpretation of visual cues, body language, or sound. It is a study of not only what a symbol implies, but also how a symbol got its meaning and how it functions to make meaning in society.

Rune

I Ching hexagram

Chinese love symbol

ENERGY FIELDS

Many ancient cultures believed that invisible energy flows through everything and that it can be harnessed for healing or beneficial purposes. By tapping into this "subtle energy," we can find lost objects, read people's minds, or look into the future. Subtle energy also refers to the medium through which our conscious will influences both animate and inanimate matter. Still baffled by exactly what this energy is, scientists think it may be a field of energy beyond the known frequencies of the electromagnetic spectrum. Energy researcher Cleve Backster (b. 1924) demonstrated how human emotions can affect the cells of plants and vegetables. He experimented with white blood cells taken from a human donor, and whose emotions continued to influence the reactions of the plant cells even at a distance. Known as the Backster Effect, this is similar to the "morphogenic field concept" put forward by British biologist Rupert Sheldrake (b. 1942), who theorized that an intention-laden force field is transmitted from one being to another via an "unknown" force.

HOW DOES FORTUNE TELLING WORK?

According to many esoteric traditions, there is a connecting force that permeates all existence. This connection includes the "random" shuffling of cards, or choosing a rune from a bag. The belief that life is "causal," in other words, that the only connection between two events is because one caused the other, is a modern scientific viewpoint. There is a far more ancient belief that everything in the universe is interconnected, and that patterns in the zodiac or a teacup, or events or actions in a person's life, are all part of an invisible force.

The great twentieth-century psychologist Carl Jung coined the word "synchronicity." This term describes the experience of events that are not causally related, but occur together in a way that becomes meaningful to the person experiencing them. An example might be a chance encounter with an old friend in the street, after which you discover you were actually thinking about each other that morning. Jung was fascinated by all forms of divination, and believed that the I Ching, Tarot, and astrology were examples of synchronicity at work. He believed that the tarot card we select, for example,

is prompted by something inner that needs to be expressed or must become manifest in the outer world, and to alert you to the fact that the card you chose has meaning for you.

The patterns and symbols involved in fortune telling are the keys to the door to this mysterious force. If we learn to work with our psychic sense or intuition too, we can align with this universal force to read into the future.

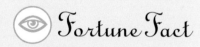

Fortune Fact

The seemingly random choice of card or oracle at one moment is a powerful significator of the meaning of that moment. It is almost as if the card or rune picks you as you pick it.

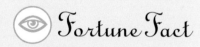

LEARNING TO USE YOUR INTUITION

THE SIXTH SENSE AND FORTUNE TELLING

Carl Jung defined intuition as an "irrational function using perception via the unconscious." The word "intuition" comes from a Latin word that can be roughly translated as "to look inside." There are many other terms used for intuition, such as ESP or extrasensory perception, the sixth sense, and more commonly a hunch, feeling, or gut instinct. Most people recognize intuition as a sudden fleeting moment of awareness, or sometimes a complete "knowing." Sometimes it happens so quickly that you miss what it is you "know." It's almost as if you know something without knowing how you know!

Scientists and psychologists conclude that intuition is a right-brain function, fueled by an emotional trigger. The left brain is responsible for logical thinking and the right brain for feelings and creativity. Scientists believe that a good feeling implies you're going in the right direction. However, this doesn't take into account why the emotion is triggered in the first place. The fortune teller's approach is that the sixth sense is an instant connection to the universal storehouse of knowledge.

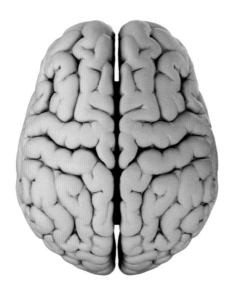

EXERCISE TO IMPROVE YOUR INTUITION

FIRST ORACLE READING

This simple but fun way to consult an oracle and to "read your future" relies on your intuition and will help tone up its power. Many people use a book as an oracle, like the Bible, *The Complete Works of Shakespeare*, or a favorite collection of poems or stories. This is the most basic way of divining the future.

Find a favorite book and go to a quiet place; sit down and relax. With the book in front of you, close your eyes and riffle through the pages back and forth. As you do so, think of a simple question, like "What will my day be like?" or "Who will be important for me today?" Or just think of the day ahead and what you would like to achieve.

Now stop at a page that "feels" right to you, and without looking, place your finger on the page and begin to run it across the page and then stop, when you "know" this is the place.

Now open your eyes and read the words nearest or beneath your finger. They may make up a phrase or sentence, or just be one or two words, but there will be "something" that makes you know that these are the right words.

Throughout the day, keep a note of how the words have relevance to you: maybe the people you meet, the events that happen, the things people say. You will find some amazing "synchronicity."

FORTUNE-TELLING TOOLS

Personal fortune telling is a time-honored way of accessing your deepest knowledge. The techniques in this book can help you look to the present and the future to increase your self-knowledge, ease decision-making, and plan for greater success and happiness. The fortune-telling methods and tools serve as a bridge between everyday reality and all that lies beyond the veil of the tangible. But it is not just the tarot cards or the runes that are giving you answers. The cards, runes, or I Ching wake you up to the symbolist world view, so that when you add your own personal intuitive powers to the equation, your fortune-telling skills will be incredible.

The universal psychic power channels through the person who rolls the dice, reads the palms, deals the cards, or peers into the crystal ball. The power doesn't belong to a diviner any more than to a healer. But as soon as you learn to read the symbols and open your intuitive sense, you become a conduit for expressing this mysterious universal language. Then you can use the knowledge for wisdom, future happiness, and to help others to make choices and determine their own future, too.

Whether you prefer tarot cards or consulting the I Ching, there are fortune-telling tools here to keep you entertained and most of all, to enjoy. You can concentrate just on one chapter, or combine several methods of divination when you are a little more practiced. There may be one technique to which you're immediately attracted: don't feel you have to start with the Tarot and finish with candle wax patterns, nor follow the order of the chapters. Delve in and see which symbols inspire you. Some will give you that moment of "knowing"; others, you may not like.

No one technique is more difficult than another, it's all a matter of personal choice. Above all, trust in yourself, take control of your destiny, and good fortune will be yours.

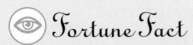 Fortune Fact

Esoteric author Ray Grasse believes that people are returning to a "symbolist" world view, one that was shared by many ancient cultures such as the Chinese Taoists, early Greek philosophers such as Heraclitus, and later Hermetic Renaissance thinkers such as Paracelsus, Cornelius Agrippa, and Dr. John Dee. This is a way of perceiving the universe as all phenomena being interwoven, linked by symbols and correspondences.

THE SECRET LANGUAGE OF THE TAROT

WHAT IS THE TAROT?

*T*arot is a deck of seventy-eight cards rich in symbolism and imagery. Each card has a name, number, and specific image, which work together to create the card's meaning. The Tarot is quite simply a universal language that is spoken through the use of archetypal symbols.

An archetype is a quality, essence, or blueprint; an original model of behavior, personality, feelings, experience, or idea. Throughout history, certain words, symbols, or codes have been used to describe these archetypes. According to psychoanalyst Carl Jung, we all resonate to these symbols because they are carried in both our personal and collective unconscious. The latter is a great universal sea of knowledge we can all tap into via the Tarot.

By getting to know the meaning of the tarot symbols and your own reaction to those images you can work with them in a positive way to tell your own fortune and those of others. However, if you look for negative answers, you'll find them. If you choose to look for positive answers and a positive future, then you will succeed. Working with the Tarot is also about learning to respect the old fortune teller's saying, "What goes around, comes around," or "What you give out to the universe, you'll get back tenfold." Learning the tarot language is meant to be a joy, not a pain.

The Tarot is used not only for fortune telling, but also for self-understanding, personal growth, and the ability to make positive choices for the future. As you learn the language of the Tarot, you can take a card every morning to see what kind of day you will have, or even imagine a favorite card in your mind when you want something to happen.

BEHIND THE SIGNS

Dark Associations

With the rise of Christianity, everything pagan was considered to be the work of the devil, including most divinatory methods such as the Tarot. These associations still remain in the murky waters of our unconscious, but nowadays the Tarot is more accepted as an ancient pathway to understanding more about yourself and your desires, which can be harnessed to enhance your life journey. The Tarot is neither a belief nor a creed; it is simply a tool for revealing what is, and what will be.

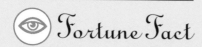

Fortune Fact

The Tarot has often been likened to a mirror; it reflects us at any given moment in time, and so what we see in the mirror, or the Tarot, is ourselves. But it's up to you to interpret honestly and see the objective mirror image for what it is, whether you like the truth or not.

ORIGINAL SYMBOLS

The Tarot has always been shrouded in mystery. It is thought to have originated several thousand years ago in ancient Egypt, when places such as Giza and Abydos were centers for mystical practice and the worship of gods. Symbols were created to produce a secret language only known to initiates of these mysteries.

The word "tarot" is a secret word all of its own. Antoine de Gebelin, an eighteenth-century French linguist and freemason, believed it was derived from the name of the Egyptian god of wisdom and words, *Thoth*. He suggested that the twenty-two main cards were based on an ancient set of tablets of mystical wisdom, saved from the ruins of a burning temple. This "Book of Thoth" outlined a secret language in which all gods could be contacted through hieroglyphs and numbers. He also discovered that the hieroglyph "*tar*" meant "way" or "road," and "*ro*" or "*ros*" meant "king"; put together—the "royal road of life." From stone carvings, there is evidence of sets of "Thoth" tablets used by pharaohs to discover their future. Many scholars agree that after the Greeks conquered Alexandria, mystics and seers from Egypt translated these hieroglyphics into images that could be understood in Europe.

Some nineteenth-century scholars preferred to believe that the word "Tarot" is partly formed from an anagram of the Latin word "*rota*," meaning a wheel. In occult circles, "*rota*" means the eternal ending and beginning of cycles of change, as revealed through tarot card readings.

Over the centuries, fascination turned to skepticism and fear, and the Tarot has only recently come back into favor. It is now seen as a symbolic book, pathway, or mirror of opportunity, to be read as a journal of your chosen lifestyle and future desires.

BEHIND THE SIGNS

Top Trumps

In the Middle Ages, a card game known as "*tarocchino*" or "*tarocchi*" – and known today as "trumps" – was played in Italy. It is likely it was influenced by the tarot decks used by the court seers and astrologers, rather than the other way around.

THE DECK'S STRUCTURE

The Tarot is made up of twenty-two main cards, known as the Major Arcana, and four suits of fourteen cards, called the Minor Arcana. The twenty-two Major Arcana cards represent universal archetypes, while the Minor Arcana represent the way these manifest in daily life. The Major Arcana are qualities that flow through all of us, while the other fifty-six cards are events, people, activities, and things that go on in life. *Arcana* is the Latin plural of *arcanum*, meaning "secret." So Major and Minor Arcana mean "big secrets" and "little secrets."

The word "arcana" is also linked to the Latin word *arca*. An arca was a Roman box, usually full of secret things. When you first start using the Tarot, imagine you are looking down into a treasure chest, and taking out its secrets one by one.

HOW TO READ THE SYMBOLS

There are no "rules" to reading the Tarot, other than using both the symbols and your own intuition to develop the story laid out before you in the cards. In the following chapters there is a brief interpretation you can work with to help you read the cards.

Like any language, the Tarot is rich in different "words" or symbols. As a beginner, you'll find it easier if you use word associations to help you with the images. For example, some of the most simple symbols throughout history have been the Sun and the Moon. The Sun is associated with daytime, energy, light, power, glory, the hero, champions, and happiness; the Moon with night, darkness, emotion, fear, and warning.

Take your time, look at one card for a while, and see where its images take you. For example, take out the card called The Sun. Here, you see the sun shining, a little child happy upon a horse, sunflowers in the

XIX

The Sun

background, a scene of happy days, and a sense of enlightenment. Even the horse is happy, as the child is confident on its back. If you shut your eyes and imagine a horse, what kind of horse do you see? Is it a fine stallion or a quiet pony? What kind of child do you see? Does it make you remember your own childhood with regret, anger, or delight? We all project our individual concerns onto what we see, which is why, when we read the Tarot, we must be careful we don't think wishfully, or only see what we want to see.

THE CHANGING FACE OF TAROT

Many different styles of tarot cards have been developed over the centuries.

In the Renaissance, with a renewed interest in ancient esoteric mysteries, a significant number of tarot decks were developed in Italy, such as the exquisite Visconti-Sforza deck, painted for the fifteenth-century duke of Milan.

The eighteenth-century French linguist and freemason Antoine de Gebelin developed his own set of seventy-eight cards, on which most decks have since been based.

At the end of the nineteenth century, an occult scholar, Arthur Edward Waite, developed his own set of tarot cards, believing that each card embodied universal truths or archetypes. The Rider-Waite Deck was painted by his friend Pamela

Colman Smith, a fellow member of the Order of the Golden Dawn mystical society. It has become one of the favorite tarot decks used today, famous for its pictorial representations of each of the numbered cards in an easy-to-interpret style.

Twentieth-century occultist Aleister Crowley created a wonderful tarot deck that was designed and painted during the Second World War a few years before his death in 1947. The Thoth or Crowley deck, as it is known, is highly popular and rich in alchemical symbolism.

It's important to choose a deck you really like. Today, there are many available, from the Marseilles, Rider-Waite, and Universal decks, to the more recent Mythic Deck and the Crystal Tarot. For beginners, I recommend the Universal Deck or Rider-Waite, as both have specific images for all the numbered cards.

Caring for Your Deck

Keep your tarot cards in a special box or pouch. You can even wrap them up in a silk scarf, but when you first take them out of their box, lay them out on the table to clear away any negative energy from their journey to your home. Each time you use them, either return them to their box, or place them in the pouch. If you do a reading with someone who themselves seems very negative, perform this little ritual after the reading to clear their difficult energy away. Place the deck face down on your table, and tap the top card twice with your finger. Turn the deck over and tap the now bottom, face-up card twice with your finger.

SHUFFLING

Shuffling requires some practice as the cards are a lot larger than normal playing cards.

The simplest way to shuffle is to place the deck of cards face down on the floor or table, spread them out and move them around until they are all mixed up. Then you can gradually build up piles of random cards, still face down. Finally, put them altogether in one stack, and then cut them three times. Often, however, the cards will end up a mixture of reversed and upright, and as a beginner you will then need to turn the reversed cards the right way up. This makes for much easier interpretation when you first start doing layouts.

A second way to shuffle, which will keep the cards all the same way up, is to drop cards that are in your writing hand between cards held loosely in your other hand. Keep shuffling until the cards are well mixed up, then cut the pack three times, face down.

DRAWING AND CHOOSING A CARD

Fan the cards out in one hand if you can, and with the other hand, run your finger along them until one speaks to you. Alternatively, lay the pack face down on the table, and fan the cards out into an overlapping long row in front of you until you can see all the edges. Then run your finger along the row of cards until a card "speaks" to you.

WHAT TO ASK

Many people think the cards will just give you answers to the future without asking anything in particular, and of course they can. But ask specific questions so that you learn to interpret the cards in relation to that question. Avoid asking judgmental questions such as, "Should I end this relationship" or "Why is my boyfriend so unkind?" Instead, rephrase as "I have a problem in my relationship; how can I improve it?" or "My life is very dull; what career change would help?"

THE MAJOR ARCANA

GETTING TO KNOW THE TAROT CARDS

*T*he twenty-two Major Arcana cards are the twenty-two major symbols that
thread through our lives as qualities, emotions, feelings, and archetypal
energies. As you start to look at each card in turn, think about how you react
to it. Does the Death card make you shiver with fear? Does the Tower worry you?
What does the Chariot really mean? All the qualities of these cards are hidden
deep within us, so when we react, we are reacting to our own unconscious values
and judgments on these qualities. As you learn to understand them, you learn
to understand yourself, too. As you draw a card at random, observe not only the
images, numbers, and keywords, but also your feelings.

Name

The name of each card is given below the picture. The names can be ideas or experiences, such as Strength and Judgment, or they can be various people, such as the High Priestess or the Empress. The Moon, the Sun, and the Star are other ways of representing qualities, and these are ancient archetypal symbols, hidden deep within us.

Number

Each card has a number. Numbers, as you will see in the numerology chapter, have special qualities, too. It was believed by the ancients that numbers were associated with specific stars and constellations. All the numbers have a mystical significance associated with their corresponding tarot card.

Imagery

All cards have powerful imagery. Whether it's the collapse of the Tower, the Lovers together, or the dog howling at the Moon, as soon as you see these images a feeling or quality is evoked. Detailed symbols are also explained, such as why is there a lion, halo, serpent, angel, ram's head, mountains, half-moon, or pillars, and what do they signify?

Zodiac Affinity

Each card corresponds to a zodiac sign or planet. This also gives you a clue to the meaning of the card.

Keyword

Every card is given keywords and a key phrase to help you with immediate interpretation, followed by a more detailed interpretation. It is up to you to work with these ideas and develop them in relation to your own questions or issues.

BEHIND THE SIGNS

One-card Answers

Ask a question, one where you know the response can only be "yes" or "no." For example, "Will I have new romance this weekend?" Shuffle the cards, then pull one from the deck, or run your fingers along the deck until you feel a card "jumps" or "calls" at you to be taken. Look at the card and if it is an even-numbered card, say the two of Wands, then this is a positive affirmation; if it is an odd number, say the Magician, being number 1, then it is a negative.

GETTING TO KNOW THE CARDS

The best way to understand the language of the Tarot is to start looking at the Major Arcana cards first. If you take your time to study each card, it's rather like reading a book. The most basic qualities are all represented here at a universal level.

First Reading

When you start reading the cards, it's easiest not to do complicated spreads, or ask difficult questions. Sometimes it's best to do just an open reading, which allows your own intuitive skills to come into play and gets your mind exercised and working with symbols and images.

Open Readings

Open readings are when we just pull a card, or lay out cards in a simple pattern and see what they say without asking any questions. This is useful for choosing a card for the day ahead or just getting some insight into your current choices.

One-card Answer

You can ask a question, or just pull a card to confirm your feelings or intuition about something, then look up the interpretation and relate it to your problem.

Storytelling

One of the best ways to get to know the cards is to make up a story around the character or imagery of the card. What is the Fool doing, for example? Where is he going, why is a dog barking at his feet, and so on?

THE FOOL

Astrology key: Uranus
Number: 0
Keyword: Adventure
Key phrase: Ready to take a risk
What you see: A young man walks toward the edge of a cliff without looking where he is going.
Interpretation: The fool is an eternal optimist. He is smart, even though it looks as if he might walk over the cliff edge. We imagine the worst; he does not. The fool represents new beginnings, unconventional life quests, and the urge to leap in at the deep end. He reminds us that resistance is sometimes more foolish than risk. The card also means taking a leap in the dark, falling suddenly in love.

The Fool

THE MAGICIAN

Astrology key: Mercury
Number: 1
Keyword: Manifestation
Key phrase: Putting ideas into action
What you see: A magician stands before a table. He holds a wand in one hand pointing to the sky, and points to earth with the other.
Interpretation: This card implies you are ready to achieve a goal, manifest your dreams, or have the potential to merge ideas with practical arrangements. This card indicates you're a bit of a miracle-worker; it's time to juggle with ideas, adapt to changing circumstances, and be ready to persuade others of your plans.

The Magician

THE HIGH PRIESTESS

Astrology key: The Moon
Number: 2
Keyword: Secrets
Key phrase: Trust hidden feelings
What you see: A woman sits holding a scroll on her lap between two pillars, a crescent moon at her feet, a cross round her neck, and a veil hides a secret place.
Interpretation: A secret is about to be revealed, either one of your own or from someone close to you. Alternatively, a wise woman will influence you.

✪ *In Renaissance versions of the Tarot, the High Priestess was often known as "Pope Joan." According to a legend, Joan was an English girl who eloped with a monk, disguised as one herself. The monk was murdered on their journey to Rome, so she carried on alone and eventually became a cardinal. Just as she was about to become the pope, she gave birth to a child on the steps of St Peter's and died.* ✪

The High Priestess

THE EMPRESS

Astrology key: Venus
Number: 3
Keyword: Abundance
Key phrase: Creative or material reward
What you see: A woman sits in a chair amidst the lush countryside. She wears long full robes, hinting at her pregnancy.
Interpretation: When you draw this card, you can be sure of getting results in any plan. It also implies you are about to mother someone or something in some way. This card can often suggest you are about to be influenced by an earth mother type, or that you are about to gain creative reward and feel good about life.

The Empress

THE EMPEROR

Astrology key: Aries
Number: 4
Keyword: Authority
Key phrase: Taking control of a situation
What you see: A man dressed in rich robes. He sits upon a throne, surveying all that he owns.
Interpretation: Whenever you choose this card, it suggests it's time to organize your life and you can now make headway with your plans. It can imply that someone in authority will be an influence in your life, but mostly that if you take control of a situation, assert your desires, you will get what you want.

The Emperor

THE HIEROPHANT

Astrology key: Taurus
Number: 5
Keyword: Knowledge
Key phrase: Doing what's expected of you
What you see: A priest sits between two pillars.
Interpretation: This card simply represents being influenced by a religious figure or someone from a traditional establishment. When you draw this card as a daily card, for example, you need to conform to what others are saying, or listen to good advice from a guru, trustworthy colleague or friend. This card can also imply meeting someone who will try to change your beliefs or opinions.

✪ *The word "Hierophant" is from an ancient Greek word meaning "a teacher of ancient mysteries." These were often magicians from the East or mystics, priests, and philosophers.* ✪

The Hierophant

THE LOVERS

Astrology key: Gemini
Number: 6
Keyword: Love
Key phrase: Choice and commitment
What you see: Two naked lovers are looked on by an angel, or sometimes by Cupid. In some decks there is a third person in the scene, as if a choice must be made.
Interpretation: The simplest way to interpret this card is that it means a love relationship will be hugely influential to you right now, and that in the future you may have to make an important choice or a commitment.

✪ *In the Lovers card, a serpent clings to a tree, reminding us of the biblical tale of Adam and Eve. The symbol of snakes and lovers is universal and suggests that sexual temptation and desire is more powerful than we think.* ✪

VI

The Lovers

THE CHARIOT

Astrology key: Cancer
Number: 7
Keyword: Willpower
Key phrase: Control over your emotions
What you see: A young charioteer in a chariot with starry curtains is led by two sphinxes as they leave a turreted city behind.
Interpretation: This card suggests there may be conflicting thoughts or feelings in your life, and you're finding it hard to listen to your head. The chariot implies it's time to persevere; don't let your emotions sway you into making a decision. Assert yourself; whatever your mission, only you can make it happen.

VII

The Chariot

STRENGTH

Astrology key: Leo
Number: 8
Keyword: Courage
Key phrase: Gentle persuasion
What you see: A young woman gently holds open a roaring lion's mouth. In some decks the image suggests she is carefully closing the lion's jaws.
Interpretation: Gentle force is needed now to resolve a situation. When you draw this card, it is time to take responsibility for your actions, and show tolerance and compassion to others and yourself. This card often indicates that courage and facing reality will bring you the changes you truly want.

✪ *In some decks the Strength card is placed at number 11, and Justice at number 8. The beautiful imagery of the lion and the lady in the Visconti deck places Strength at 8 because 8 symbolizes control, power, and taming of the senses.* ✪

VIII

Strength

THE HERMIT

Astrology key: Virgo
Number: 9
Keyword: Soul-searching
Key phrase: Looking for direction
What you see: A hermit contemplates the light of his solitary lamp in a barren landscape. It is as if he is looking back and reflecting on his own past.
Interpretation: Time to reflect carefully before you make a choice. This card often means that you must look within yourself for wisdom. Also, that looking back to the past for answers may help you resolve a current problem. In the future, you may need to take a long hard look before committing yourself. This card really means that you need to do some soul-searching to discover the truth.

IX

The Hermit

THE WHEEL OF FORTUNE

Astrology key: Jupiter
Number: 10
Keyword: Beginning
Key phrase: A turning point
What you see: A huge wheel turns in the sky, surrounded by mythical beasts.
Interpretation: The Wheel of Fortune represents the changing cycles in our lives, and how we are influenced both by apparent "fate" and by our own free will. There will now be choices to be made, new journeys begun, and the chance to jump on the bandwagon. Don't resist the changing cycles; embrace the new and make personal progress.

The Wheel of Fortune

JUSTICE

Astrology key: Libra
Number: 11
Keyword: Balance
Key phrase: Logical decision-making
What you see: A woman acts as judge. She sits on a chair carrying a set of scales and a sword.
Interpretation: This card represents balance and authority, logic and objectivity. Whenever you draw this card, you are being asked to think rationally before making any decision. You should not be judgmental about other people's opinions. Sometimes this card means you will be influenced by legal issues, and there is hope of a successful outcome in your favor.

Justice

THE HANGED MAN

Astrology key: Neptune
Number: 12
Keyword: Sacrifice
Key phrase: Seeing the truth from a new angle
What you see: A man hangs from a tree by his foot, a halo around his head. He is alive and seems happy.
Interpretation: This card reminds you that if you do something you hadn't anticipated doing, you are most likely to get good results. In fact, like the upside-down man, seeing things from a very different angle is the answer to success. It means you may have to give up an old belief, idea, or feeling, but learning to let go will bring you happiness. You will no longer be in limbo and can move on.

XII

The Hanged Man

DEATH

Astrology key: Scorpio
Number: 13
Keyword: Change
Key phrase: Closing one door, opening another
What you see: A skeleton in armor rides a horse in triumph across a battleground. In the background, the Sun rises behind a ruined city, and a pope prays that Death won't scythe him down.
Interpretation: This card spooks most people, but it is not scary if you know its true meaning: that it's time to let go of the past and start again. Death represents the parting of ways, the closing of doors, the dumping of emotional baggage. Inevitable change means that other doors will open, new emotions will bring you happiness, and so will new encounters. Change is often fearful, but if you embrace it, you will discover it will embrace you back with love, too.

XIII

Death

TEMPERANCE

Astrology key: Sagittarius
Number: 14
Keyword: Compromise
Key phrase: Moderation creates success
What you see: An angel or goddess pours water from one goblet to another. She walks through a pond filled with irises.
Interpretation: It's time to balance out the two "cups of feeling" in your life. These represent desire and common sense. Sometimes we can get led astray by one or the other. This means compromising, accepting someone else's viewpoint, or moderating your own desires. By accepting that your common sense says one thing, and your desire says another, you can work out a compromise to give value to both.

Temperance

⭐ *Iris was the Greek goddess of the rainbow. She was the goddess who linked the sky with the earth, and took messages from mortals to the gods.* ⭐

THE DEVIL

Astrology key: Capricorn
Number: 15
Keyword: Illusion
Key phrase: Being bound by your fears
What you see: We see the devil and two naked people chained to his cave.
Interpretation: When you draw the devil, you are chained to your illusions about love, money, or power. Also, look to your own inner devil—the one who causes you to react without thinking, to demand too much, to get obsessed with negative thinking or silly behavior. It's time to look at your own dark side and acknowledge it. You may be bound by a narrow perception, believe you will fail or can't do something, or fear the unknown. When we finally accept we may be living a lie, then we can free ourselves from the devil's chains.

The Devil

THE TOWER

Astrology key: Mars
Number: 16
Keyword: Disruption
Key phrase: Unexpected event or challenge
What you see: A tower is struck by lightning; people fall from the turret as a fire rages within.
Interpretation: The Tower represents structure in our personal world. But the lightning symbolizes unexpected or external events that happen to change our lives, or force us to rethink our lives. This card indicates that it's time to adjust quickly to change. It will be for the better, but you must accept the challenge and chaos around you. There may need to be a breakdown of an old way of living or thinking to allow you to move on.

The Tower

THE STAR

Astrology key: Aquarius
Number: 17
Keyword: Realization
Key phrase: Seeing the light
What you see: A maiden pours water into a stream from two jugs. There are stars in the sky, and the landscape is calm and peaceful.
Interpretation: The ancients used the stars to navigate by, and when you see the star card you know that you too can trust in the universe to help you manifest your goals. This card always implies progress, renewed self-confidence, and a time for inspiration.

The Star

THE MOON

Astrology key: Pisces
Number: 18
Keyword: Confusion
Key phrase: Changing feelings
What you see: The Moon casts her ghostly light over a barren landscape, where dogs bark, a crayfish rises from a pool, and a road seems to lead nowhere in the distance.
Interpretation: The Moon's cycles are always shifting and changing, from new to full, and to new again. This card represents these shifts of energy in your life, and how confusing and sometimes unpredictable your feelings can be, too. Listen to your intuition; a friend or future admirer may not be trustworthy.

✪ *The Moon has always been symbolic of the dark side of life, associated with feelings, emotions, and the feminine, while the Sun is symbolic of masculine energy, ego, light, and courage.* ✪

The Moon

THE SUN

Astrology key: The Sun
Number: 19
Keyword: Joy
Key phrase: Being happy and carefree
What you see: A child rides a horse while the sun shines down and sunflowers bloom.
Interpretation: This card represents all that is light, confident, and positive. Like the sun, you too can shine and bring happiness to those around you. There is a child in you that needs to play, and when you draw this card it suggests you will soon be having as much fun as you want.

The Sun

JUDGMENT

Astrology key: Pluto
Number: 20
Keyword: Liberation
Key phrase: Reevaluation and acceptance
What you see: An angel blows a trumpet, calling on the dead to rise up and be reborn.
Interpretation: This card means it's time to wake up and liberate yourself from the past. This card always says you can now drop old values, and accept new ones. Very soon, the weight of guilt, self-sabotage, or blame will be taken off your shoulders and it will be time to start afresh.

XX

Judgment

THE WORLD

Astrology key: Saturn
Number: 21
Keyword: Fulfillment
Key phrase: Accomplishing your dream
What you see: A naked lady dances in the center of a flower garland, while mythical beasts surround her.
Interpretation: When you see the World, you know this is going to be a time when the world is your oyster. It's time to complete a project or be rewarded for something. What you can do now is feel good about yourself, and be at one with the universe.

XXI

The World

THE MINOR ARCANA

GETTING TO KNOW THE TAROT CARDS

he Minor Arcana, or four suits of "small secrets," is made up of four different energies, each one representing a state of being: swords represent our state of mind; cups our emotions and feelings; pentacles our day-to-day and active life; and wands our visions, imagination, and desires. These aspects of ourselves often manifest in the world around us when we are not acting out the quality in ourselves. For example, you may be always falling in love with free-spirited individuals who don't want to be tied down. The Knight of Wands represents this energy, but it is also in you. Each suit is made up of ten numbered cards and four "court" cards—the page, knight, queen, and king.

The Numbered Cards

In many of the older decks, the numbered cards are often just shown with a certain number of the "pips" or symbols of the suit. But since the Rider-Waite deck was created in the late nineteenth century, its use of pictorial pip cards started a fashion that means that most modern decks have pictures to help you to read the cards more easily. All you need to learn is the number, suit, and keyword associated with each card to get you started.

The Court Cards

The court cards do not have a hierarchy as in playing cards. In fact, the king is sometimes not as powerful an energy as the knight, for example. The king, queen, knight, and page all represent the qualities of people you might meet in your day-to-day life, but also that you can find in yourself.

The king represents dynamic, masculine energy. King types often appear in your life as authority figures, fathers, strong leaders, or men with a mission.

The queen represents feminine energy, and queen types can appear as mother figures, bossy women, or females in powerful roles.

Knights represent the best and worst of the qualities of the suit. For example, the Knight of Cups is an utter romantic, but also elusive and untrustworthy.

Pages represent the playful spirit of the suit, so the Page of Pentacles, for example, might turn up in your life as a financial whizz kid.

Although these qualities may manifest as people, they may just be acting out a role for you at the time of a reading to indicate what might be missing in your own life, or what needs to be activated.

BEHIND THE SIGNS

The Four Suits

Swords represent our state of mind. They tell us how our concepts and ideas direct our life and how we can mentally block or create situations from our thoughts.

Cups represent our emotions, feelings, and needs. They show the deeper levels of our instincts and intuition and reveal that sometimes we must follow our heart, not our head.

Pentacles represent our day-to-day and active life. They reveal how we go about making a success of our world and the reality of our situations.

Wands represent our visions, dreams, imagination, and desires. When we draw Wand cards, we are being asked to look at what we truly want.

Number Meanings

The keywords for the numbers given below are a useful starting point for interpreting the suit cards:

Ace or One – Beginning
Two – Negotiation
Three – Communication
Four – Control
Five – Creativity
Six – Understanding
Seven – Intuition
Eight – Power
Nine – Action
Ten – Transition

THE SUIT OF SWORDS

Swords describe our state of mind and reveal how we paradoxically rely on rational thought to solve our emotional problems. When we draw a Sword card, it reminds us that our head and heart must work together.

Ace of Swords

Keyword: Honesty
Key phrases: Facing the facts. Knowing the answer. A time to resolve a problem.
Interpretation: Prioritize your ideas and you'll reach a satisfactory solution to any difficulty. Conflict and challenge may be necessary to create beneficial change.

Two of Swords

Keyword: Denial
Key phrases: Blocked feelings. Being unavailable. Living a lie. Blind to the truth.
Interpretation: You are pretending indifference or are split off from your feelings, hoping they'll go away. Someone is refusing to make a choice.

Three of Swords

Keyword: Wounding
Key phrases: Discovering a painful truth. Betrayal. Hurting someone else.
Interpretation: Time to let go of old conflicts and clear away the past. Even if it hurts, the wound will soon heal and you can move on to better times.

Four of Swords

Keyword: Contemplation
Key phrases: Coming to terms with things. Taking time out to make a decision.
Interpretation: Don't let anyone else push you for an answer. Now is the time to take a step back, reflect alone, and find the truth for yourself.

Five of Swords

Keyword: Acceptance

Key phrases: Time to let go of your fears. A willingness to accept change.

Interpretation: You are not sure if you can accept your limitations, but it's time to conquer your self-doubt, and be realistic about your goals.

Six of Swords

Keyword: Recovery

Key phrases: Moving out of troubled waters. Getting over difficulties.

Interpretation: You're now about to move forward and see the way ahead. You'll soon be more positive about life and this marks the beginning of a new you.

Seven of Swords

Keyword: Deception

Key phrases: Fooling others or yourself. Getting away with it.

Interpretation: Don't run away from a situation or deceive yourself about your actions. Time to use stealthy tactics with rivals.

Eight of Swords

Keyword: Restriction

Key phrases: Feeling trapped. Waiting to be rescued. Floundering in your feelings.

Interpretation: You feel stuck in a situation that you have no control over. All it takes is a change of perspective, clear thinking, and positive direction.

Nine of Swords

Keyword: Worry

Key phrases: Overwhelmed by thoughts. Sleepless nights and obsessive thinking.

Interpretation: Realize that you need to search deep inside and you will wake up to exactly what it is that is worrying you and deal with it.

Ten of Swords

Keyword: Enlightenment

Key phrases: Turning point. Cutting through illusions.

Interpretation: Time to say goodbye to the old you and welcome in the new. Things can only get better if you realize that the sun is about to shine upon you.

Page of Swords

Keyword: Foresight

Key phrases: Refreshing honesty. A young-at-heart person. Challenges ahead.

Interpretation: Time for new ideas based on basic thoughts and experience. This card can also imply you will meet someone who is an intellectual challenge.

Knight of Swords

Keyword: Impetuous

Key phrases: Fascinating or life-changing encounter. Your own rash behavior.

Interpretation: You may get involved with a madcap, lively person who won't take no for an answer. This can be you, too; tactless, impatient, and chaotic.

Queen of Swords

Keyword: Determination

Key phrases: Upfront and direct. Not afraid to say no. A quick thinker.

Interpretation: This card represents either someone in your life who is strong and determined to move on, or it can reveal your own ability to think astutely and to get results.

King of Swords

Keyword: Assertive

Key phrases: Get to grips with a situation. Adept and strong-minded.

Interpretation: An influential figure who has authority and strength and who knows how to handle affairs in an honorable way. It may be that your assertive nature will get you results.

 Fortune Fact

Swords are associated with the element of Air in astrology and the zodiac signs Gemini, Libra, and Aquarius.

THE SUIT OF CUPS

When we draw a Cup card, we are being asked to feel what the power of love really means to us. The suit of Cups is concerned with feelings and emotions. The cards are usually associated with relationship issues.

Ace of Cups

Keyword: Romance

Key phrases: New love. Infatuation. Establishing a new bond.

Interpretation: A gift of love awaits you. Either you are about to fall in love, or someone will fall for you.

Two of Cups

Keyword: Attraction

Key phrases: Harmony and cooperation. Mutual attraction. Sexual union.

Interpretation: You are about to merge closely with someone, whether in physical or emotional ways.

Three of Cups

Keyword: Celebration

Key phrases: New friends. Enjoying your social life. Sharing your happiness.

Interpretation: A time of celebration, whether in love, a marriage, or the birth of a child. Time to enjoy socializing with like-minded people.

Four of Cups

Keyword: Frustration

Key phrases: Not being able to make a choice. Focusing on the bad.

Interpretation: You are going through a negative phase and can only see what's wrong in your life. The good things are out there, so open your eyes and see what's being offered to you.

Five of Cups

Keyword: Loss

Key phrases: Regrets over lost opportunities. Feeling emotionally confused.

Interpretation: You are still wishing things had been different, but all is not lost. Time to move on and, in your loss, find something to gain.

Six of Cups

Keyword: Nostalgia

Key phrases: Sentimental memories. Meeting someone from the past.

Interpretation: Fond memories of the past mean you're without a care in the world. You may bump into an ex-sweetheart but will enjoy the encounter.

Seven of Cups

Keyword: Choices

Key phrases: Too many possibilities. Creative ideas in abundance. Wishful thinking.

Interpretation: There are so many choices available to you that you can't make a clear decision. It's time to think clearly and focus.

Eight of Cups

Keyword: Letting go

Key phrases: Leaving behind a difficult situation. Moving on to better things.

Interpretation: This card always indicates a time when you will move on and start again. Strike out a new route for yourself.

Nine of Cups

Keyword: Pleasure

Key phrases: Your wish will come true. Sensual indulgence.

Interpretation: You have a right to feel content and happy, and this card indicates your wishes coming true. Bask in your success, but don't let it go to your head.

Ten of Cups

Keyword: Fulfillment

Key phrases: Family happiness. Sexual completion. Feeling at one with the world.

Interpretation: A great time for peace, love, and harmony. Prepare yourself for some emotional joy and the promise of security.

Page of Cups

Keyword: Birth

Key phrases: New relationship. Birth of a child. A younger lover or flirtatious admirer.

Interpretation: Traditionally tells of the birth of a child. A younger lover coming into your life. Expect new romance.

Knight of Cups

Keyword: Rescue

Key phrases: Dashing off to rescue someone. Being rescued by love. Exaggerated feelings.

Interpretation: You may be about to sweep someone off their feet, or be swept off your feet yourself. You may be falling in love with someone who is not available or having extremes of feeling about two different people. Are you in love with love, and have you got your romantic desires out of all proportion?

Queen of Cups

Keyword: Compassion

Key phrases: Unconditional love. Willing to help others.

Interpretation: A kind person may enter your life to remind you of your own compassion. This card also indicates being loved for your warm heart.

King of Cups

Keyword: Maturity

Key phrases: Acting from emotional knowledge. Accepting limitations. Awareness of human nature.

Interpretation: You are emotionally mature enough to make a decision. Your calm approach will be of benefit to others. A stabilizing person is about to enter your life.

 **Fortune Fact**

The suit of Cups is linked to the element of Water in astrology and the signs Cancer, Scorpio, and Pisces.

THE SUIT OF PENTACLES

The suit of Pentacles is concerned with the tangible world and our perception of it. It represents the reality we create around us and the people or things that shape us. When we draw a pentacle card, we are being asked to think about what influence the material world has on us and how we interact with it.

Ace of Pentacles

Keyword: Gain

Key phrases: Reward for effort. Starting a new business.

Interpretation: This card reveals you will be successful in any new undertaking, as long as it is a valid scheme.

Two of Pentacles

Keyword: Juggling

Key phrases: Dealing with several problems at once. Fluctuating fortunes.

Interpretation: You can now show how adaptable you are and have the flexibility to deal with money issues. Be open to change and you'll succeed.

Three of Pentacles

Keyword: Skill

Key phrases: Building up a reputation. Getting on with the job. Professional growth.

Interpretation: This card indicates that your plans are progressing. Not only have you shown your creative skill, you are beginning to make headway, too.

Four of Pentacles

Keyword: Possessive

Key phrases: Refusing to budge. Not taking a risk. Controlling others with money.

Interpretation: Without taking a risk, nothing can be gained. Time to step out of your comfort zone.

Five of Pentacles

Keyword: Lack

Key phrases: Financial or material loss. Feeling like a victim. Neglecting your needs.

Interpretation: You are feeling unlucky, lost, and even a bit of a victim. You may have money problems, everyone does, but it's time to see the glass as half full, rather than half empty.

Six of Pentacles

Keyword: Generosity

Key phrases: Willingness to give. Being considerate. Gaining something from a loss.

Interpretation: A time when you feel quite benevolent. Just take care you aren't using kindness to have power over someone.

Seven of Pentacles

Keyword: Evaluation

Key phrases: Where to go from here? Taking stock of your achievements.

Interpretation: There is a choice to be made. Do you take the tried and trusted route or follow an unknown road? The adventure might take you to greater things.

Eight of Pentacles

Keyword: Persevere

Key phrases: Profitable venture. New set of learning skills. Dedication to a job.

Interpretation: Your enthusiasm for a project or new wisdom can now propel you to achieve greater things.

Nine of Pentacles

Keyword: Accomplishment

Key phrases: Enduring sense of achievement. Pleasure and material success.

Interpretation: You feel good about yourself. Being self-reliant and proud of what you do will pave the way to a great future.

 Fortune Fact

The suit of Pentacles is associated with the element of Earth in astrology and the zodiac signs Taurus, Virgo, and Capricorn. Pentacles are sometimes called "Coins" and represented merchants, trading, and wealth in the early tarot decks.

Ten of Pentacles

Keyword: Affluence

Key phrases: Enjoying wealth. Putting down roots. Stability and security.

Interpretation: Your need for a sense of permanence or traditional family life is top of your agenda.

The Page of Pentacles

Keyword: New project

Key phrases: Slow but valuable progress. Realistic aims. Taking one step at a time.

Interpretation: Involve yourself with a new project and it will work for you now.

The Knight of Pentacles

Keyword: Hardworking

Key phrases: Dedicated to getting the job done.

Interpretation: Someone who is intent on finishing a project, but in a slow and methodical way. You'll get to what you are aiming for, but it will take hard work.

The Queen of Pentacles

Keyword: Sensible

Key phrases: Reliable and loyal. A realistic outlook on life. An earth mother.

Interpretation: A practical person will influence you to be more resourceful and get results.

The King of Pentacles

Keyword: Achievement

Key phrases: Enterprise and initiative. Competent and responsible.

Interpretation: An achiever or a business or financial adviser with the Midas touch. You're about to go through a period when you can be one step ahead of the game.

THE SUIT OF WANDS

The suit of Wands represents creative energy and how we go out into the world seeking, exploring, and imagining the future. Wands represent our desires and dreams; whether we can manifest them depends on other cards in a layout. When you draw a Wand card, you are being asked to take a more positive look at life, to direct your energy into activating your dreams.

Ace of Wands

Keyword: Inspiration
Key phrases: A great idea. A solution to a problem. Knowing the way forward.
Interpretation: This card asks you to act on your great thoughts and do something about them. You now have innovative and enthusiastic ideas.

Two of Wands

Keyword: Pioneering
Key phrases: Widening your perception. Going the distance. Sensing your power.
Interpretation: Courage to achieve your goals. Time to be a pioneer in whatever you do. Take a risk without fear and prove your point.

Three of Wands

Keyword: Adventure
Key phrases: Seeking the truth. Starting another journey. Exploring the possibilities.
Interpretation: It's time to use your gift of foresight to lead you down a new road and follow up on a hunch or feeling. You know what's best for you.

Four of Wands

Keyword: Celebration
Key phrases: Freeing yourself from the past. Spontaneous love. Freer than a bird.
Interpretation: A time to celebrate your achievements or take a break from hard work and dream of the future. A time for celebrating life.

Five of Wands

Keyword: Struggle

Key phrases: Feeling frustrated about events. Irritating problems holding you back.

Interpretation: People are trying to stop you reaching your goals. Soon you will get back to normal if you just take a deep breath and smile.

Six of Wands

Keyword: Promotion

Key phrases: Feeling as if you've succeeded. Triumph and victory.

Interpretation: A high level of success and even public acclaim. You are about to be the center of attention, but remember, "pride comes before a fall."

Seven of Wands

Keyword: Defiance

Key phrases: Sticking to what you believe is right. Proving yourself.

Interpretation: Stand your ground and show you deserve to be where you are. You may have critics or have to decide if something is worth fighting for.

Eight of Wands

Keyword: Excitement

Key phrases: Quick developments and action needed. Getting things done.

Interpretation: Look out for exciting news. Take a fresh approach to your plans and get ready for action. Sort out your priorities and move forward.

Nine of Wands

Keyword: Preparation

Key phrases: Ready for anything. Defending your beliefs. Persistence and awareness.

Interpretation: You now have the determination to overcome any obstacle. This is your chance to prove you're untouchable.

Ten of Wands

Keyword: Struggle

Key phrases: Taking on too much. Having the strength to endure an uphill struggle.

Interpretation: Don't give in, even if it feels like a burden. You will win at all costs, but make sure the price is not too high.

The Page of Wands

Keyword: Creativity

Key phrases: Fresh ideas and insight. A charming messenger.

Interpretation: When you draw this card, either you are about to start a new, exciting venture, or meet someone young, charming, and optimistic who will have a good influence on your future plans.

Knight of Wands

Keyword: Adventure

Key phrases: A seductive invitation. A change of residence. A journey into the unknown.

Interpretation: The Knight of Wands can turn up in your life as a passionate but unreliable stranger. It can imply you will fall in love suddenly, become reckless, or express your own daring streak. Sometimes this card can mean you are about to travel or move home.

Queen of Wands

Keyword: Charisma

Key phrases: Self-assured, accomplished. A woman who knows what she wants. Confident and undaunted.

Interpretation: A confident woman is going to be of great influence in your life. It can also imply that your own charisma will now be expressed.

King of Wands

Keyword: Bold

Key phrases: Inspirational authority figure. Role model. A powerful leader.

Interpretation: Show off your abilities and prove you're good at what you do. This card can also imply that a man in power can help you achieve your current goals.

HOW TO READ THE CARDS

USING THE TAROT

*T*here are many different ways of using the Tarot. You can draw one card in the morning to see what kind of day you will have or do a full spread using anything from two cards to twenty. On the following pages are some different layouts you can try to start you off. As you develop your intuition, get to know the cards, and begin to realize how revealing the spreads can be, you can also start to invent your own layouts. When you get more experience you can create layouts to reveal hidden issues or what someone else is feeling or thinking about you. You can also look at your relationships in detail or discover what a whole year ahead is going to be like, using one card for each month.

The Chariot

The Tower

STEP-BY-STEP GUIDE

1. Shuffle the cards in one of the recommended ways on p. 26 and cut three times. As you shuffle, focus on your question or desire.
2. Place the deck face down on the table and gradually spread the cards out into a long line in front of you, still face down.
3. Close your eyes and run your finger along the line of cards until you feel ready to choose one card. You may have a flash of intuition about a card or just feel the moment is right. Don't rush it, just let your mind be open to the energy.
4. When you have chosen a card, place it FACE DOWN in the first position shown in whichever diagram you are using (see pp. 58–65). Continue choosing and placing cards in positions as shown.
5. Next, turn the first card you placed down face up. If it is upside down, place it the right way round. (Reversed cards require more advanced tarot readings.)
6. Look at the card and think about what it might mean before you look up the interpretations given, then turn over the other cards one by one.

When you are more experienced, you'll be able to combine the meanings of all the cards and eventually read the spread without even thinking about it, as if reading the words in a book.

WHAT'S HAPPENING IN MY LIFE TODAY?

Here's a first simple spread to get you going. You can use this spread on a daily basis to see what kind of day you might have or what issues might be important for you right now. With just a few cards you will quickly learn to read the symbols and interpret the imagery.

For this layout, you can use just the Major Arcana cards. Keep them separate from the Minor Arcana. Then, once you've got used to these twenty-two cards, you can move on to more detailed readings by using all the cards. In the next few pages are some more layouts to gradually give you larger spreads with more versatile readings.

You only need three cards for this, so lay out the cards in the order shown in the diagram.

1. The important issue of the day
2. What needs attention
3. Influence for the future

SAMPLE READING:

1. The Emperor. The important issue today will center around an authority figure who will seem rather powerful.
2. The Star. What needs attention is to keep faithful to my long-term dream and not to be led astray.
3. Strength. The influence for the future will be that I am emotionally strong and will not allow someone to direct my life or change my mind about my desires.

Result: You know that today you will meet a strong personality who might sway you from your goals; don't listen—stick to your personal views.

IV

The Emperor

XVII

The Star

VIII

Strength

PROBLEM AND SOLUTION SPREAD

This is another simple spread to try out with only a few cards, again using the Major Arcana only. You can use this spread any time you have a problem that you feel you can't work out alone.

1. The problem
2. How it is influencing you
3. How to resolve the problem
4. The outcome

SAMPLE READING:

1. The Tower. Changes in your life are making you worried, and you're not sure how to deal with them; you may be going through a break-up, or fear that your relationship is going to end.

2. The Devil. You are attaching yourself to the past, trying not to see how to work things out. You are being influenced by family expectations. Are they your own?

3. The Hanged Man. You can resolve the problem by changing your viewpoint, seeing your problem from a different perspective.

4. The World. Things will get better and soon you will realize that the problem was all in your mind. Time to travel, move on, or find happiness again with your partner.

1 XVI

The Tower

2 XV

The Devil

3 VII

The Hanged Man

4 XXI

The World

HOW TO READ THE CARDS

THE DESTINY SPREAD

This spread uses both the Major Arcana and the Minor Arcana.

1. You now
2. The current problem
3. Future benefits
4. The future outcome

SAMPLE READING:

1. **The Fool.** Right now, you want to take a risk or leap in at the deep end of a new project.
2. **Five of Wands.** You fear your partner or colleagues won't listen or will try to put you down.
3. **The Emperor.** A man in power will help you.
4. **Three of Cups.** With realistic expectations, you'll soon be celebrating your new venture.

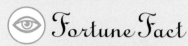

Fortune Fact

The word "destiny" comes from an old French twelfth-century word "destiner," meaning to be fated. This is from an earlier Latin word, "destinare"—to make fast.

HOW TO FIND NEW ROMANCE SPREAD

There are times when you can use the tarot cards to indicate not only if you will meet someone new, but also how you will find new romance. This spread tells you what you must do to enable new love to come into your life, and in what way you will meet someone. Again, use all the cards.

1. You now
2. What you seek
3. What you must express
4. What you must give
5. What you must look for
6. Where you will find new romance

SAMPLE READING:

1. **The Seven of Swords.** You're deceiving yourself about what you want. Time to be honest with yourself.
2. **Justice.** What you really seek is a harmonious relationship, where you can be equal.
3. **Eight of Pentacles.** Show that you are willing to work hard at a relationship.
4. **The Empress.** Give out true compassion and affection; don't pretend to be something you're not.
5. **Ten of Cups.** What you must look for is the kind of person who is committed and serious about love, someone who is mature and knows how important family is to you.
6. **The Queen of Wands.** You will find love or new romance through a charismatic friend, colleague, or business contact.

THE HORSESHOE SPREAD

This five-card spread is useful if you have a specific question. It looks simply at what you can expect, and even tells you what the unexpected elements of your short-term future will be! This well-known gypsy layout has been used for centuries, and is useful for a quick reading for answering the question over the coming month or even week.

As always, lay the cards out in the order of the diagram, face down. Then, turn them over to reveal each card one by one. The best way to interpret the cards is to do each one before you turn the next card over, so you're not influenced by the other cards.

1. You now
2. The expected
3. The unexpected
4. The immediate future
5. The outcome

Example question: *I'm at a crossroads in my career. What shall I do?*

SAMPLE READING

1. The Moon. You're currently confused, but listen to your intuition about what direction you need to follow.
2. The Lovers. You expect making a choice will be hard or even dependent on someone else.
3. The Seven of Wands. You will have to stick up for yourself when challenged by someone, and then you will know exactly what you want to do.
4. The Three of Pentacles. You take on a new skill and discover a new pathway.
5. The Hierophant. An important advisor, guru, or mentor will take notice and help you to forge ahead with your plans.

11 TEN

Wands

10 ONE

Cups

9 TWO

Pentacles

8 KNIGHT

Wands

7 TWO

Swords

12 X

The Wheel of Fortune

THE ZODIAC SPREAD

This simple spread uses twelve cards, but it gives you an idea of the kind of experiences you will have in the next month in different areas of your life. For example, you can find out what kind of home life you will have; whether your love life will be easy or problematic; whether you will travel; or whether friends and money will be tying you down!

As before, lay the cards out one by one as in the diagram. Don't turn any over until you have finished laying them out.

6 EIGHT

Cups

1 XIV

Temperance

2 ONE

Swords

3 XIX

The Sun

4 VII

The Chariot

5 II

The High Priestess

1. Your quest for the month ahead
2. Money
3. Friends
4. Family/home
5. Romance
6. Energy levels
7. Love
8. Sexuality
9. Travel
10. Career
11. Social life
12. The past

SAMPLE READING:

1. **Temperance.** Time to moderate your goals, be patient for results, be more casual about life, and enjoy.
2. **Ace of Swords.** An innovative idea could help you make more money.
3. **The Sun.** Happy days ahead, with lots of fun and childlike enthusiasm.
4. **The Chariot.** You need to take control, or family and domestic issues could get out of hand.
5. **The High Priestess.** A secret is revealed.
6. **Eight of Cups.** You need a change of scenery; get out and about and work on a new exercise plan.
7. **Two of Swords.** You find it hard to get close to someone.
8. **Knight of Wands.** You want to express your sexual needs.
9. **Two of Pentacles.** Take short trips to satisfy everyone's wishes.
10. **Ace of Cups.** Emotional satisfaction comes from an unexpected opportunity.
11. **Ten of Wands.** You feel overwhelmed by commitments; take some time out alone.
12. **The Wheel of Fortune.** An encounter with someone from the past gives you insight into future desires.

BEHIND THE SIGNS

The Houses of the Zodiac

The zodiac spread is based on the twelve "houses" of the zodiac. These are twelve segments of the chart that govern various areas of your life. When planets enter these "houses" we find that they influence that specific part of our life. When tarot cards replace the planets, we can immediately see what's coming up for us in the coming month. This spread was often used by astrologers and seers of the Italian nobility to plot and scheme against their rivals or enemies.

PALMISTRY

YOUR HAND—A UNIQUE LANGUAGE

*F*or thousands of years, we have tried to tell our fortunes by looking for patterns, shapes, and symbols not only in nature, but on and even in our own bodies, too. Heads, hands, faces, and of course "body language" all have a unique story to tell about each of us as individuals. Palmistry is the art of reading your fortune from the lines in the palm of your hand. The language of the lines, shapes of hands, fingers, thumbs, and the mounts on the hands tell you more about yourself than you would ever think. Lines, like words, can reveal deep truths, and if you stick to the old traditional interpretations of palmistry, you can discover much about your own potential qualities and destiny.

LANGUAGE OF LINES AND SHAPES

There are four basic hand shapes associated with the four elements of astrology: Earth, Fire, Air, and Water. The shape of your hand indicates the general style of your character, and it will not really change over the course of your lifetime. The length, breadth, and shape of your fingers and thumbs reveal more about your personality, as do your finger lengths in relation to your thumbs, and so on. The "mounts" are the soft pads under each of the fingers, as well as other specific areas of the palms. These will reinforce the language of the lines and shapes to give you a more detailed character analysis.

The language of your hand is unique, but like any book, the words are accessible to everyone who reads that language. The lines, bumps, shapes, and mounts have a universal meaning that everyone shares, but what makes your hand special is that, like fingerprints and your birth horoscope, each hand is different: it is a unique blueprint of you.

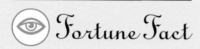

Fortune Fact

The lines on our hands change as we age, reflecting external events and experiences and the available potentials throughout our life journey.

BEHIND THE SIGNS

Which Hand Is Which

There is some confusion about which hand means what. But now that being left-handed isn't thought to be the work of the devil, it is the hand you write with, or the hand you use most, that is considered your main (major) hand. The other (minor) hand is usually thought to reveal your hidden talents, and what you really, deep down inside, are searching for. The main hand reveals your life journey as it unfolds, your quirks and behavior, or the events and influences to expect in the future.

BRIEF HISTORY

The practice of palmistry can be traced back to the ancient cultures of India, China, and Egypt, threading its way to Europe via ancient Greece about the fourth century BCE. Known first as "chiromancy," it was mentioned by Hippocrates, Plato, and Aristotle, and later, in Roman times, by Pliny and the Emperor Hadrian. The first known texts in medieval Europe were written about 1160 when Christian mystic John of Salisbury discussed the magical arts, noting, "the *chiromantici* are those who presage the hidden aspects of things from the inspection of the hands."

The Digby Roll IV, a manuscript in scroll form dated 1440, recounts information about hand-reading and reveals that it was a common practice during the Renaissance. But the growing power of the Church and its persecution of anything pagan forced all forms of divination underground, and it wasn't until the nineteenth century that fortune telling became a popular pastime in the home. Fraudsters and skeptics took advantage of the craze, and palmistry fell into disrepute. Recently, it has become a serious study of character and future potential.

Cheiro

The well-known predictive palm-reader Cheiro was born in 1866. An Irishman by birth, he was also known as Count Louis Hamon. He gained a massive popular reputation because of his psychic gifts but mostly because he knew all the right people! He read the hands of Prince Edward, the Prince of Wales, General Kitchener, William Gladstone, and Joseph Chamberlain, as well as literary and artistic figures such as Mark Twain, Sarah Bernhardt, and Oscar Wilde.

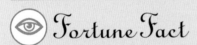

Fortune Fact

In 350 BCE, Greek philosopher Aristotle wrote that palmistry "is a judgment made of the conditions, inclinations, and fortunes of men and women, from their various lines and characters which Nature has imprinted in the hands."

HOW TO READ A HAND

1. First look at the general shape of your hand. Does it resemble the diagrams of the Fire, Earth, Air, and Water type hands on pp. 70–71 in any way? Read the interpretations for those hand shapes and see if your character fits the description.

2. Look at your "main" hand—i.e. your writing hand. Feel the bumps, the mounts, look at the shape of your fingers, check out the brief interpretations, and make a few notes on paper to keep you focused and objective.

3. What do you want to know? If you are interested in finding out about career, then look at the head and fate lines; if you're interested in relationships, then look at the heart line; if you want to know about your true potential and lifestyle journey, look at the life line.

4. Make notes according to the interpretations given on the following pages. You will discover contradictions along the way, but then that is the nature of personality. Your hand is an extension of all your personal inconsistencies. Some of us can be carefree one minute, maybe gloomy the next.

5. Remember, the lines on your hands alter as you get older. These reflect the changing events, unconscious desires (minor hand), and available potentials.

6. As you make notes and add keywords, jot down negative and positive qualities. What you are reading is a map of yourself.

7. Finally, draw the outline of your own hand on paper (use your minor hand to draw around your major hand), then fill in the shape of your lines and write keywords by each line.

HAND SHAPES

The shape of your hand tells you about your basic character. The four main shapes are all linked to the astrological elements, Fire, Earth, Air, and Water.

To discover the basic shape of your hand, hold it up in front of you, palm facing you, and compare it with the illustrations below to see which shape is closest to yours.

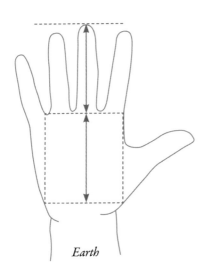

Earth

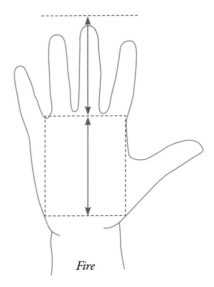

Fire

THE PRACTICAL HAND
Astrological affinity: Earth
Shape: Square palm, short fingers
Keywords: Practical, sensible
Reliable and down-to-earth, you are realistic and take pride in your appearance and tastes. Loving and loyal, you could do well in all kinds of creative work, and have practical abilities that others envy. You thrive on challenges and are motivated to succeed and live a good, materially secure life. You take relationships seriously, and prefer long-term commitment to brief flings.

THE SPIRITED HAND
Astrological affinity: Fire
Shape: Long, oblong palm with medium-length fingers
Keywords: Animated, restless
You thrive on adventure and exploring new opportunities. If you're not out and about, or passionate about some cause, you are quick to find a new challenge. You just want to get on with life and live it, and you need a busy social lifestyle, physical exercise, and mental stimulation. In love relationships, you can be impulsive and impatient; you need your freedom and don't like being tied down.

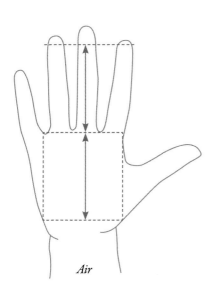

Air

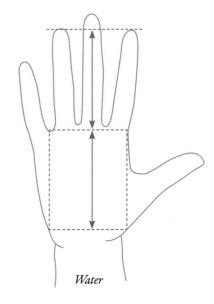

Water

THE INTELLECTUAL HAND

Astrological affinity: Air

Shape: A squarish palm with long tapering fingers (all about the same length)

Keywords: Idealistic, communicative

You are a thinker first, a doer second. You have a brilliant mind, and with a logical and positive outlook on life, you inspire people around you. Research work or transmitting information of any kind suits you, and you have a highly objective and optimistic approach to life, making you able to go with the flow. Romantic and idealistic, you can feel totally out of your depth in love relationships.

THE SENSITIVE HAND

Astrological affinity: Water

Shape: Narrow, slim palm, long slim fingers (third finger usually much longer than the others)

Keywords: Creative, emotional

Dreamy and unrealistic, you escape into your imagination and can be hugely successful in any artistic, musical, or creative work. Generous and compassionate, you often empathize too strongly with others and get overwhelmed by the energy around you. Your intuition is powerful, so trust it, rather than others who lead you astray. Romantic and needy, you often get involved in secret love affairs.

FINGERS AND THUMBS

Your fingers and thumbs have shapes of their own. Try not to look at your nails, as long nails can disguise the overall shape of your fingers. Look for the most common shape, as digits can be a mix of long, short, thin, and thick.Fingers and thumbs tell you what kind of work will suit you best.

THE THUMB

Thumbs represent the energy you give out and whether you are a self-starter, freelancer, hermit, born leader, or someone who needs to follow the herd.

Short or small thumb

Usually only reaching the bottom of the first digit. You are quiet and need a passive, stress-free environment. You don't like making key decisions, so work behind the scenes.

Long, slender, conic-shaped thumb

Usually reaches almost to, or is longer than, the middle line of the digit finger. Creative, idealistic, and talented, you express your ideas well, but need to work with a team to help you ground them.

Square-ended thumb

You are highly self-motivated and need to lead from the top to express all your great powers of initiative and persuasion.

Bulbous or squat thumb

Working alone suits you best, and then you truly get things done. You may be better off working freelance.

FINGERTIPS

Check which of these shapes occurs the most in your remaining nine fingers.

Conical fingertips (rounded at end)

You quickly work out what people are thinking or feeling and would be suited to working in the health or healing professions.

Pointed fingertips

Taste and style matter to you. You have an eye for design, color, and beauty, and you would do well in the fashion, music, art, and creative fields.

Square-ended fingertips

You're a natural moneymaker and highly professional. The best sectors for you are property, finance, and managerial, where you can seal a deal.

Spatulate fingertips (flat, spreading)

You thrive on the natural world, so you'd be great working in gardens, countryside, the great outdoors, or traveling the world.

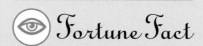

Fortune Fact

Bill Gates has an Air hand, which shows his broad and objective perspective on life. With conic tips to three of his five digits and the thumb, he's an idealist and wants to make a difference to the world.

MOUNTS

The mounts are the soft, spongy pads under the base of each finger and other areas of the palm. Some people have fleshier mounts than others, simply because they have thicker hands or fuller muscles.

The mounts are named after the eight original planets in astrology, with each planet representing a Roman god: Jupiter was the god of the sky, Venus the goddess of love, Mars of war, Saturn of the Earth, Apollo of light, Mercury of trade, Neptune of the oceans, and the Moon of emotions.

THE EIGHT MOUNTS

1. The Mount of Jupiter
Found under the first finger (next to the thumb), well-developed Jupiter mounts show confidence, ambition, idealism, and determination to succeed.

2. The Mount of Saturn
Under the middle finger. Well-developed Saturn mounts indicate a balanced, realistic outlook on life.

3. The Mount of Apollo
Located at the base of the third, or ring, finger. Creativity, compassion, and self-confidence are indicated if this mount is well-developed.

4. The Mount of Mercury
Found under the little finger, well-developed Mercury mounts indicate a great communicator.

5. The Mount of Venus
The fleshy area at the base of the thumb. A well-developed or rounded Mount of Venus means you enjoy the pleasures of life; family and home are important, too.

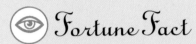 **Fortune Fact**

People with very long palms and fingers can have surprisingly large mounts, such as Michelle Obama, whose large Sun mount reveals her to be a positive-thinking person, strong-willed, but highly creative. Well-developed mounts reveal that this particular quality will be strong in someone's life.

6. The Mount of Neptune
This can be found toward the base of the palm, right in the middle. When this is well developed, the owner is acutely sensitive to the needs and feelings of others.

7. The Mounts of Mars
There are two Mars mounts, just below the digit mounts crossing the upper part of the palm. If this area is well developed, then you are energetic, impulsive, and enthusiastic, but often take too many risks.

8. The Mount of the Moon
The lunar mount is located between the little finger and the wrist, on the outer edge of the palm. A well-developed lunar mount signifies creativity.

THE MINOR HAND

In this book, the minor hand is used to determine your hidden self and unlock your talents and potentials.

1. Look at your minor hand and make a note of any differences to your major hand, particularly the overall shapes of fingers, palms, and lines.

2. The lines will probably reveal the biggest differences. Maybe some are fainter or stronger. It is this difference that will reveal your secret desires or talents that you need to develop.

SAMPLE READING:
Your minor hand fate line is longer and stronger than your main hand's fate line. This would mean that on the surface you aren't particularly ambitious or clear of your direction (main line—thin, faint, or short) but because on your minor hand it's long, powerful, and deeper, you need to express your need for a vocation, and find something that gives you a purpose.

BEHIND THE SIGNS

Reading Between the Lines

Many palm readers literally read between the lines on your hand, too. They look at spots, moles, freckles, ridges, tiny fine lines, scars, and skin variations. These all change as we age. There is an old belief that any tiny horizontal lines located just below your little finger on the outside of your hand will tell you how many children you will have.

INTERPRETING THE LINES

The four main lines are the life, heart, head, and fate lines.

1. **The life line** describes your life journey and lifestyle
2. **The heart line** tells you about your love life and relationships
3. **The head line** tells you how your mind works
4. **The destiny line** reveals career direction

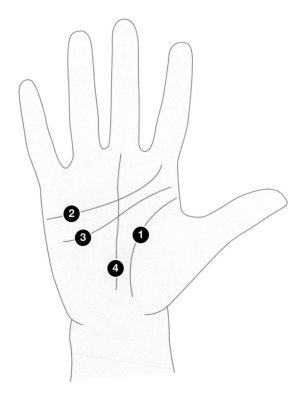

THE LIFE LINE

This line starts above the thumb and curves round toward the wrist, usually around the Mount of Venus. There are many variations of the curves; some even fork as they reach the bottom. Here is an interpretation of the most common types of life line.

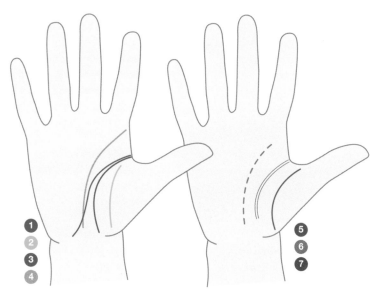

1. Curves in a wide arch toward middle of hand
You want a big life with loads of travel, adventure, and independence. You want to be different from everyone else.

2. Stays close to thumb
You're a home-lover; not particularly ambitious, but you yearn for a settled family life.

3. Veers at end toward outside of wrist
You will probably move abroad, or spend most of your life living far from home.

4. Line starts from index finger
Strong-willed, you need a varied lifestyle where events, people, and experiences are always changing.

5. Cuts through the Mount of Venus
You live a very limited life, or under the influence of others, such as your family or partner.

6. Breaks in the line
Many changes in your life, but it's you who will be making the decisions.

7. Double life line
Two lines very close and parallel to each other. You lead a double life, maybe commute between two different countries, or have two lovers, two jobs, or two lifestyles.

THE HEART LINE

This line starts at the outer edge of your palm beneath your little finger and curves across or sometimes lies straight across the rest of the palm.

Variations:

1. Strong, well-defined line, no breaks

Love affairs are key themes in your life. You are determined to make love work for you and are loyal and true.

2. Short, thin, or weak

Indicates you are not really sure about your feelings. You may seek approval to validate who you are. Sex may be more important to you than emotional involvement.

3. Starts high close to little finger and stays at top of hand

More interested in the intellectual side of relating. You are very self-critical and need to be less defensive in love. You need a good intellectual rapport and no emotional scenes.

4. Starts low beneath the outside knuckle of palm

Romantic and idealistic, you fall in love too quickly and demand too much from your lover. You often feel let down when romance fades and can flit between partners to rekindle the magic.

5. Line ends between first and second finger

Passionate and seductive, you make it clear who's in charge of the relationship. You exude charisma and will have many admirers or lovers. You can be loyal if you meet your match.

6. Ends beneath second finger

Conventional relationships matter to you. Long-term love is more important than affairs, and you're good at building a successful working relationship.

7. Ends beneath first finger

Open and free-spirited, you like your freedom and don't want to be trapped or lead a conventional love life. You are a friend as well as a lover.

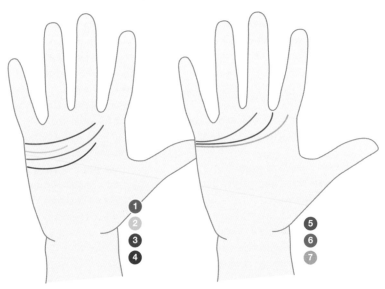

THE HEAD LINE

This line is found usually about midway between the heart and life line. It starts between the thumb and first finger and runs across the center of the palm. A wide line implies you're methodical and want to get things done. If it's thin or faint, you may find it hard to make decisions.

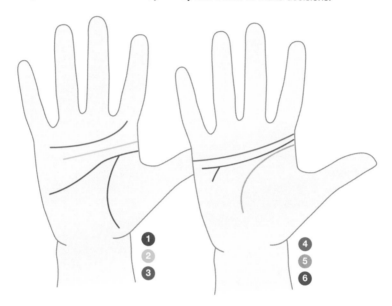

1. Head and life line joined at the start

When young you have little confidence and your family influence is strong. But later, you compensate by becoming obsessively independent and ambitious.

2. Head line separate from life line

A radical thinker, you get on in life and don't care what others think about you. You rely on yourself and rarely ask for help.

3. Line rises just under index finger

Competitive and motivated, you believe you have luck on your side, and you usually do. You are confident and competitive and adore challenges. Larger than life, you exude great intellect and presence.

4. Line is straight across palm without curving

Material security is important to you. You care about the way you look and think in a focused and careful way to make sure you take total control of your life.

5. Head line curves downward toward Mount of the Moon

You are extremely imaginative, sensitive, and creative; you like to work alone where you can develop your own ideas and prove you're a genius.

6. Ends in a fork

If the line splits at the end, this is a sign of a born writer or communicator. A particularly dominant or large fork means you will likely have public success as a journalist or an author.

THE DESTINY LINE

The line of career and vocation starts from a point somewhere near the bottom of the palm and runs vertically or diagonally upward to the base of the fingers.

1. Line runs straight from middle bottom to top of palm and ends beneath middle finger with no breaks

This is the line of success and good fortune, as long as you dedicate yourself to your career, you know what you want, and where you're going.

2. Line begins on Mount of the Moon and curves up to middle or fourth finger

You need to break away from conventional expectations and travel or live abroad. You're independent and need a career where you're always learning something new.

3. Line veers toward first finger

Often the sign of a true leader. You will receive much acclaim for your work. Best suited to running your own business, but you could also stand out from the crowd if other lines indicate your road to fame.

4. Line faint, or short

You're not very ambitious and need a laid-back environment where pressure, achievement, and success aren't the only things in life. You work best in a team, with friends, animals, or behind the scenes.

5. Breaks in the line

Many career changes, so be prepared for ups and downs, and for success to come and go. You have an extraordinary talent for adapting to new challenges, and you're flexible enough to take on any role. Good for acting, or working in creative industries where you can go with the flow.

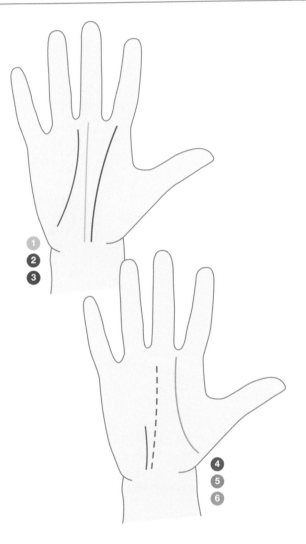

6. Line starts very close to Mount of Venus

You aren't very ambitious and prefer to work from home, or in the family business. You may take up a career that a parent has chosen for you without really knowing what you want. Depending on your other lines, you may be a secret achiever, so check out the balance of all your hand to see if you're repressing truly ambitious desires!

CELEBRITY HANDS

Picasso's long, straight destiny line crossed his hand completely, from bottom to top. According to Vedic palmistry, a line starting from the wrist indicates a continuation from a vocation started in a previous life, suggesting that Picasso was a born artist.

Kate Middleton's curving heart line almost reaches between her index and her middle finger, showing that she can be loyal and true, but is definitely the boss in her marriage to Prince William.

Albert Einstein's head line was separated from his life line, which gave him independent thinking. His head line reached the Mount of the Moon, and he reportedly found many of his ideas through his intuition. When he was trying to solve a problem he would play the violin and wait for inspiration.

Oprah Winfrey has a strong life line circling the Mount of Venus without any break. This indicates an abundance of energy. Starting on the Mount of Jupiter, it shows that Oprah wants things to be done her way.

THE LANGUAGE OF NUMEROLOGY

WHAT IS NUMEROLOGY?

Numbers have a language of their own and have been considered powerful symbols of universal energy ever since the ancient Babylonians, Chinese, Greeks, Egyptians, and Hebrews developed their own unique systems of using numbers to divine the future. The father of modern-day Western numerology is Greek philosopher and mathematician Pythagoras. According to Pythagoras, numbers vibrate to the harmonics of the cosmos. The ancient Greek concept of the "music of the spheres" described how the heavenly bodies worked together in harmony. Their music, or harmonic vibrations, kept the universe working and weaving through our lives. Everything in the universe could be reduced to a one-digit number, which was the true vibrational force or music of that number.

HOW TO USE NUMEROLOGY

You can use numbers to discover whether a new partner, workplace address, home address, or potential lover will be in harmony with your own numerical vibration. All you have to do is some simple addition based on the alphabetical values of your name and the numbers of your birth date to discover your life purpose, your future, and your character.

Often, we find that one number seems to crop up for us throughout our life. For example, you may find you always see the number five on doors and cars, or there are always five people in the train with you. You may find that a number is always the same for your address, or you have two favorite friends, two favorite books, two favorite lovers!

THE PYTHAGOREAN ALPHABET SYSTEM

The numerical language was encoded into the alphabet system by Pythagoras and is the most popular way of using numerology today. Each letter of the alphabet is designated a number from one to nine. Any words, names, or whole sentences can be decoded and analyzed by using this code. To find your own specific numbers, all you have to do is add them up as suggested in the following pages and then reduce them down to one digit.

1	2	3	4	5	6	7	8	9
A	B	C	D	E	F	G	H	I
J	K	L	M	N	O	P	Q	R
S	T	U	V	W	X	Y	Z	

BEHIND THE SIGNS

Pythagoras

Most people know of Pythagoras from school geometry class. Born in 590 BCE, there is little recorded history of him. However, he set up a secret school in Italy when he was fifty. His esoteric circle of students was taught mathematics, music, and astronomy with a strict code of secrecy that they must never reveal any of his teachings. According to later historians, he was charismatic and well-loved, even winning prizes for his agility at the Olympic games.

THE BASIC MEANINGS OF THE NINE NUMBERS AND THEIR PLANET AND CRYSTAL ASSOCIATIONS

NUMBER ONE
Astrological planet:
The Sun
Lucky crystal:
Red carnelian
Keywords: Innovation, independence, beginnings, unity, summer

NUMBER TWO
Astrological planet:
The Moon
Lucky crystal:
Moonstone
Keywords: Negotiation, partnership, harmony, cooperation, yin and yang

NUMBER THREE
Astrological planet:
Jupiter
Lucky crystal:
Amethyst
Keywords: Communication, creative thinking, extrovert, spring-time

NUMBER FOUR
Astrological planet:
Uranus
Lucky crystal: Green
tourmaline
Keywords: Structure, organization, control, the four seasons

NUMBER FIVE
Astrological planet:
Mercury
Lucky crystal: Citrine
Keywords: Travel, adventure, curiosity, versatility

NUMBER SIX
Astrological planet: Venus
Lucky crystal: Turquoise
Keywords: Compassion, loyalty, family, luxury

NUMBER SEVEN
Astrological planet: Neptune
Lucky crystal: Aquamarine
Keywords: Art, music, intuition, dreamy, mystical

NUMBER EIGHT
Astrological planet:
Saturn
Lucky crystal:
Black tourmaline
Keywords: Power, proficiency, ambition, hard work

NUMBER NINE
Astrological planet: Mars
Lucky crystal:
Red coral
Keywords:
Competition, universe, visionary, outspoken

THE FOUR NUMBERS IN YOUR LIFE
There are four important numbers in your life.

Destiny number
This determines your life journey. It is worked out from your date of birth. This is a number you can't change. It tells you what you can expect to encounter in life and indicates your career pathway and natural talents.

Personality number
This is worked out from your name using the Pythagorean code. It describes your character and how you relate to other people. Of course, this number can change over the years if you decide to change your name, get given a "nickname" or shortened version of your given name, or you choose a professional name. Sometimes we don't like our given name personality, and so we unconsciously choose a name that makes us feel better about ourselves and resonates to a different number.

Secret number
This number is made up of the numerical value of only the vowels in your name. It reveals your secret desires, ideals, and what kind of lover you are.

Expression number
This is worked out using the consonants of your name only. This number describes how you express yourself and whether you're a good listener, a good talker, a social joy, or a reclusive type.

HOW TO WORK OUT
YOUR DESTINY NUMBER

This number reveals your lifestyle, the type of vocation you're best suited to, and how to be the best of yourself. As you can't change the date of your birth, work with the qualities described rather than fight against them, and you'll find you can make your life a more positive and exciting journey.

Add together all the numbers of your birth date and reduce them down to one digit. Let's say you were born on April 15, 1980. Write down the date in numerical form and then add them up like this:

$4 + 1 + 5 + 1 + 9 + 8 + 0 = 28$

Reduce this down to one digit:
$2 + 8 = 10$

And again:
$1 + 0 = 1$

So, your destiny number is **1**.

If you were born on October 15, 1989:
$1 + 0 + 1 + 5 + 1 + 9 + 8 + 9 = 34$

Reduce this down to one digit:
$3 + 4 = 7$

So, your destiny number is **7**.

Fortune Fact

Abraham Lincoln's destiny number was 5. It reveals not only that he was resourceful, magnetic, and witty, but that he had both the vision and common sense to ground his goals.

HOW TO WORK OUT
YOUR PERSONALITY NUMBER

Decide which name you prefer and are mostly known by. For example, you might have been given the name Catherine Smith at birth, but for most of your life, and because you prefer the name, you are known as Cathy Smith, or even Kate Smith. You might be married and you are now known as Cathy White. Use the name that makes you feel good to be you.

Using the Pythagorean alphabet code (p. 83), work out the numbers that relate to the letters of your name.

Look down the column to find which letter corresponds to which number, then add the numbers up, as before, and reduce them down to one digit.

For example:
Your preferred name is Cathy Smith.

Cathy
C = 3, A = 1, T = 2, H = 8, Y = 7

Now add the numbers together:
3 + 1 + 2 + 8 + 7 = 21
2 + 1 = 3

Smith
S = 1, M = 4, I = 9, T = 2, H = 8
1 + 4 + 9 + 2 + 8 = 24
2 + 4 = 6

Add the first name number to the second name number:
3 + 6 = 9

Always reduce any number over 9 down to one digit.

So the personality number for Cathy Smith is **9**.

HOW TO WORK OUT
YOUR SECRET NUMBER

Your secret number, sometimes known as the "heart" number, was traditionally worked out using the vowels in your name. This is the number of what you would secretly like to be, do, and have. It also reveals the kind of lover you are.

Write down the vowels in your name. Let's take another example, Alison Green.

A = 1, I = 9, O = 6, E = 5, E = 5
1 + 9 + 6 + 5 + 5 = 26
2 + 6 = **8**

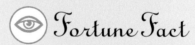

Fortune Fact

Barack Obama's secret number is 1, revealing his heartfelt desire to be some kind of celebrity—which actually came true, albeit via a political career. If you truly listen to your heart and soul, you too can realize your secret number dream.

HOW TO WORK OUT
YOUR EXPRESSION NUMBER

Your expression number describes how you go out and meet the world, how you act in public, how you interact with others in a social setting, and the sort of friendships you make.

Write down the consonants of your name.
Let's use Alison Green again.

L = 3, S = 1, N = 5, G = 7, R = 9, N = 5
3 + 1 + 5 + 7 + 9 + 5 = 30
3 + 0 = **3**

HOW TO WORK OUT
YOUR YEAR AHEAD NUMBER

Finally, this number will give you a great idea of your personal year ahead and the trends, energy, events, and opportunities that will come your way.
First work out the number for the year.

For example, let's say 2014.
2 + 0 + 1 + 4 = 7

Now add the day and month of your birth, leaving out the birth year.

So, if you were born on April 16, for example, you would add:
7 (the year number) + 4 + 1 + 6 = 18
1 + 8 = **9**

So, 2014 is going to be a number **9** year for this person.

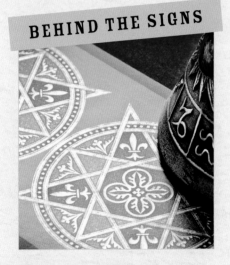

BEHIND THE SIGNS

Looking Ahead

Look at the brief key phrases for your own personal year ahead and see what kind of future you can expect.
ONE – An exciting, challenging year. Nonstop action.
TWO – New love affair, romance, or partnership. Balanced relationship.
THREE – Busy social and working life. Work hard, network, be rewarded.
FOUR – Enterprising opportunities and ambitious plans.
FIVE – Adventure, travel, moving abroad likely.
SIX – A year for settling down, feeling at home, establishing family roots.
SEVEN – Creative output and spiritual values will bring you happiness.
EIGHT – Success and power in the business world, if you have the vision.
NINE – Romantic escapades, humanitarian causes to fight for, independence.

INTERPRETING THE NUMBERS

Interpreting numbers is fun; they correspond to colors, words, images, and feelings. Here is an easy way to start getting to understand them better. Each one of the nine numbers has a separate meaning for each of the four categories. So, to help you read the language of numbers, follow the brief interpretations for the destiny, personality, secret, and expression numbers in your life.

NUMBER 1

Destiny Number

You have a pioneering spirit, and need competition, rivals, and ambitions to keep you motivated and dynamic. Your life journey will be full of challenges, but you're a born leader so make sure you work in an environment that allows you to make decisions, take control, and express your ideas.
Key potential: Be the boss, and enjoy a creative, enterprising lifestyle.

Personality Number

From when you were a baby you were probably challenging your parents, demanding food, and crying if you didn't get your way. You're a go-getter, and you prefer to do things your way, or not at all. Sometimes you can be arrogant and put other people in the back seat, but you have all the self-motivation and sparkle to be original and successful.

Secret Number

Secretly, you'd love to be in a glamorous role, a movie star or a celebrity in some way. You dominate in love relationships and would really like a sexy, spontaneous romance rather than a long-term commitment. You are a secret innovator, so unleash your wild side and show you mean business.

Expression Number

On the surface you show others that you're number one, and confident with it. Other people envy you and you often get blamed for taking risks or doing things your way without compromising.

Sean Connery • August 25, 1930

Gwyneth Paltrow • September 27, 1972

NUMBER 2

Destiny Number

A born negotiator, you're adaptable and know how to make people happy. Although you prefer to work behind the scenes, you're a great diplomat and can shine if you stand up for yourself and show you have your own opinions. Taking on a role, such as acting, can be a great way to disguise your vulnerable side.

Key potential: Choose a vocation where you can be a mediator.

Personality Number

Protective and fun to have around, you're everybody's friend. You enjoy a good social life, but you can be a bit clingy and attach yourself to your job, your past, and your family, and feel you can't do without them. Sensitive and compassionate, you need to be with someone who makes you feel wanted and adored.

Secret Number

You secretly crave emotional closeness, and deep down inside you are acutely sensitive to criticism and blame. You long to be rich, have an ideal family, and be surrounded by a beautiful home, possessions, and the luxuries of life.

Expression Number

On a one-to-one level you relate to others with ease. People find you charming, willing, and often too compromising. You are easy to confide in, but there are times when people will take advantage of your outgoing nature too.

Jennifer Aniston • February 11, 1969

Prince Charles • November 14, 1948

NUMBER 3

Destiny Number

A born communicator, you have a natural gift with words and need to express yourself in a creative way. Whether an artist, writer, or media professional, you're also an active person and need to have a variety of different outlets for your many talents. Travel, adventure, and exploring new ideas will be important throughout your life.

Key potential: Work in the media or the arts and make a career out of your creativity.

Personality Number

Bubbly and fun, you believe life's for living to the full. You're everyone's friend, but you get restless if your work or friends are dull. You prefer the unpredictable to the tried and trusted. Flirtatious and seductive, you aren't the most constant of partners, but you always adore the one you're with.

Secret Number

A secret romantic, you wish you could travel the world free of care, meet the perfect partner, and live on a desert island. Your innermost desire is to write a best-selling novel or become a philosopher.

Expression Number

Everyone thinks you're brave, confident, and full of ideas. A bit of an attention seeker, you have a busy social life and get seen in all the right places. Take advantage of your positive image and don't be afraid to follow your dream.

John Travolta • February 18, 1954

Hillary Clinton • October 26, 1947

NUMBER 4

Destiny Number

Ambitious, capable, and a born organizer, you've got what it takes to be self-sufficient and succeed at whatever you do. Practical and self-willed, your life journey will involve enterprising business opportunities and creating solid financial security for the future.

Key potential: Use your astute mind to build yourself an empire.

Personality Number

Always reliable, people know they can depend on you for help or support. You enjoy making great plans and following them through. You're often the power behind your partner's throne and are good at motivating yourself as well as others. Down-to-earth ideas and practical skills make you the perfect self-starter in any project.

Secret Number

Deep down you want to be in control of money, people, and your life. You hate change and prefer to stay with someone you don't love rather than take a risk on someone new. Secretly, you want to be an industrial spy or the head of the company.

Expression Number

Some people see you as a workaholic; others, just totally self-disciplined and trustworthy. Make use of this gift of stability and self-respect to get things done, and promote yourself in whatever career your destiny number suggests.

Nicole Kidman • June 20, 1967

Brad Pitt • December 18, 1963

NUMBER 5

Destiny Number

Witty and charming, your life journey is about travel, connections, and changing scenery. You're ready to try anything once, and all encounters, new faces, and experiences will have meaning for you. With excellent communication skills, your versatility can be put to great use in working with the public, even though you consider yourself to be a bit of a loner.

Key potential: Live abroad or work in a vocation where you are free to travel.

Personality Number

Sparkling and buzzing with ideas, you hate to be tied down and can't bear an ordinary life. You look to the next adventure and don't dwell on the past. There's always some quest you're on, and if others can't keep up with you, you'll prize your own independence. Romantic and free-spirited, you need to be with someone who's also a bit of a nomad.

Secret Number

Secretly, you'd love to travel the world and have no ties. Restless and impatient, deep down inside you want to rebel against the status quo and take a risk on a new lifestyle.

Expression Number

Friends or colleagues see you as bright, intelligent, and a bit of a risk-taker. You appear adaptable and positive about life, so use your quick-witted image to help you achieve your goals.

Mick Jagger • July 26, 1943

Angelina Jolie • June 4, 1975

NUMBER 6

Destiny Number

You like to make people feel good about themselves, and you have a natural talent for nurturing others. You prefer routine, family, and a small circle of friends and take time to get to know people before you trust them. With a generous heart, it's important you work as part of a team and be of service in some way. Your life journey will be about healing others and giving as much to the world as you take from it.

Key potential: Work with people, animals, humanitarian causes, or alternative healing to bring out your compassionate side.

Goldie Hawn • November 21, 1945

Personality Number

A great homemaker and breadwinner, you don't mind getting your hands dirty and will help anyone get out of trouble. Family and domestic harmony are important to you. Loyal and careful, you don't rush into love. You always test the emotional waters before giving your feelings away.

Secret Number

Secretly, you want a cozy home and family life, a doting partner and a simple but pleasurable lifestyle. In fact, the ordinary, conventional set-up is what you dream of, and deep inside you yearn for total emotional security.

Expression Number

People see you as delightful, charming, and easygoing. They warm to your good heart and often confide in you. Use this inside knowledge to help you get ahead in your chosen career.

Albert Einstein • March 14, 1879

NUMBER 7

Destiny Number

Psychic and almost mystical, you know that there is something else beyond the so-called reality of the world. Daydreamy and intuitive, you sometimes refuse to trust your intuition, but use it, because it is a precious gift.

Key potential: Work in music, the arts, or healing, or be creative with your psychic gifts.

Personality Number

A bit of a dreamer, you spend a lot of time alone, and others find it difficult to get close to you. You're a romantic, but find it hard to maintain long-term relationships as you need your own space too. You need a partner who will give you the time to dream and accept your changeable nature.

Secret Number

You secretly want to be a guru, healer, witch, or psychic. You know deep down that you have a powerful intuition and psychic connection to people. Liberate your psychic sense to help you follow up the goals of your destiny number.

Expression Number

Other people find it difficult to work you out, and you often get lost in thought. Sometimes you lose track of time and place and are late for dates, so admirers find you seductive and elusive but often can't be sure if they can trust you or not.

Leonardo DiCaprio • *November 11, 1974*

Julia Roberts • *October 28, 1967*

NUMBER 8

Destiny Number
You're a powerful character and are driven to succeed in life. A life journey of hard work, results, and material ambition, and one you will never give up on. You can get to the top of your chosen profession with your efficiency and innate entrepreneurial skills.
Key potential: Focus on achievement and a career where you are running your own show.

Personality Number
Self-sufficient and determined to get on in life, you often sacrifice close relationships for your career. Controlled and quick-thinking, you're also suspicious of everyone's motives and don't form many friendships, but the ones you do are for life.

Secret Number
Secretly, you desire power and material wealth. Deep down you're highly efficient and organized, even if you're not on the surface. You would adore to be a millionaire or rule the world.

Expression Number
You're always well-dressed and proud of your appearance. Others sometimes see you as bossy, but stylish and money-conscious. You can appear cool and distant, but you also have the power to mean business and prove it.

Richard Gere • August 31, 1949

Barbra Streisand • April 24, 1942

NUMBER 9

Destiny Number
A bit of a freedom-fighter, you are ready to be a champion for all kinds of causes and crusade for the rights of anything from whales to snails. You have amazing enthusiasm for new ideas and enterprises, and believe in justice for all.
Key potential: Expand your beliefs and see the bigger global picture to bring you success.

Personality Number
Honest and impulsive, you can fall in love with a stranger and the next day help the underdog at work. You need loads of freedom to roam. Romance and intrigue are more important to you than home comforts and routine relationships.

Secret Number
You secretly want to seduce your way through life, be led astray, or just live as a free spirit. You long to travel the world and have no responsibilities or ties. As you get older, let this secret dream come true.

Expression Number
Everyone sees you as lively, fun, and a genuine free spirit. Your enthusiasm is infectious and you are great to have around. When someone tries to get close to you, you hate being pinned down and don't want to get serious about anyone or anything.

Cher • May 20, 1946

Robbie Williams • February 13, 1974

LOVE COMPATIBILITY

When we meet someone for the first time, we may be able to read their body language or are attracted to them just by what they say or the way they act. But by learning to read the language of numbers, you can quickly discover someone's personality and whether they are compatible with you.

Below is a brief chart of love language by numbers. First, work out your personality numbers (see p. 87) from both your names. Then, look down the left column for your number, and along the top row for your admirer's. The box where the two meet describes the kind of relationship you can expect. For example, a three and an eight can expect a passionate relationship.

	1	2	3	4	5	6	7	8	9
1	Exciting	Indulgent	Fun	Dramatic	Creative	Moody	Unreliable	Controlling	Spirited
2	Indulgent	Serene	Sexy	Warm	Focused	Ambitious	Erratic	Successful	Steamy
3	Fun	Sexy	Hilarious	Sizzling	Wicked	Progressive	Romantic	Passionate	Adventurous
4	Dramatic	Warm	Sizzling	Calm	Arousing	Determined	Suspicious	Complete	Impressive
5	Creative	Focused	Wicked	Arousing	Madcap	Challenging	Enchanting	Carnal	Extravagant
6	Moody	Ambitious	Progressive	Determined	Challenging	Idealistic	Laid-back	Physical	Compassionate
7	Unreliable	Erratic	Romantic	Suspicious	Enchanting	Laid-back	Emotional	Provocative	Creative
8	Controlling	Successful	Passionate	Complete	Carnal	Physical	Provocative	Intense	Unpredictable
9	Spirited	Steamy	Adventurous	Impressive	Extravagant	Compassionate	Creative	Unpredictable	Wild

FORTUNE TELLING WITH RUNES

NORDIC MYTHS AND SYMBOLS

*R*unes are secret codes. In fact, the word "rune" is rooted in an old Gothic word **"runa,"** which means a mystery. Runes are usually associated with ancient Viking symbols that were carved into rocks and stones. Celtic and Norse peoples invoked the power of the gods by writing these symbols in nature. Divining runes were etched or carved on pieces of wood, and, like crystals, vibrated to a universal energy. When you are using the runes you are tapping into the harmonious vibrations of the universe to give you answers about the future. If you have a decision to make or a question you want answered, consult your runes as you would a tarot card.

Fortune Fact

The twenty-four symbolic runes are divided into three groups, each credited with special powers. Each group was named after a Norse god, those being Freyr, Heimdall, and Tyr. Freyr was the goddess of fertility, Heimdall the guardian of the gods, and Tyr the god of war.

A BRIEF HISTORY OF RUNES

The earliest Germanic tribes first used runes to enhance their magical powers or to invoke the gods. They were later adopted by the Vikings, and the fierce Norse warriors, or "berserkers," carved runes on their swords before going into battle. They believed the language of the gods would make them invincible. Large pillar stones, called standing stones, were often marked with runes to warn travelers of the power of a particular place, or had magical runic riddles, love spells, and incantations engraved on them to ward off evil. Many people carved runes on their personal items, such as combs, boxes, and jewelry, as well as on their homes as protective talismans.

According to legend, a Norse warrior called Odin, seeking wisdom and understanding of life and death, fasted with neither food nor water. Hanging for nine days and nights upside down on Yggdrasil, the tree of knowledge, his experience gave him knowledge of the runes. From that time on, aided by Viking travels, understanding of the runes spread throughout the world.

The Elder Futhark

The runes in common use today are from the "Elder Futhark." This runic alphabet was made up from the symbols most commonly used in northern Europe. The names of the runes are believed originally to be rooted in the Proto-Indo-European language that developed among the tribes who lived in the steppes of Eastern Europe on the borders of the Indian subcontinent.

RUNE BASICS

There are many different ways to cast or consult runes; a couple are shown in the following pages. You can buy many different varieties of runes these days, some made of stone or crystal, others of wood. You can even make your own by finding some small flat pebbles all about the same size and shape and drawing the runic signs on the smooth surface.

Caring for runes

Always keep your runes in a pouch or bag. Charge your runes with your own energy by carrying them around with you for a whole day and then placing them under your mattress or pillow at night.

Empowerment ritual

Do this simple traditional ritual to empower your runes with universal energy.

Lay out the runes on a cloth in the midday sun for an hour to soak up the energy of the sun.

Next, leave them face up on a window ledge at night during a full moon (it doesn't matter if there are clouds in the sky).

Write the runic alphabet on a piece of paper and then bury it in the garden.

Your runes are now activated and ready for use.

LEARNING THE LANGUAGE

Like any alphabet, it takes practice to get to know what the symbols mean. You will quickly learn to interpret each symbol with its keyword and meaning for you in the future. By using the chart on the facing page, you can get a quick sense of what each symbol represents.

THE RUNIC ALPHABET: THE SYMBOLS AND THEIR KEYWORDS

FEHU
Possessions

URUZ
Strength

THURISAZ
Challenge

ANSUZ
Message

RAIDHO
Journey

KENAZ
Clarity

GEBO
Relationship

WUNJO
Success

HAGALL
Delay

NIED
Need

ISA
Standstill

JERO
Harvest

EIHWAZ
Action

PERTH
Secret

ELHAZ
Self-control

SIGEL
Vitality

TIR
Competition

BOERC
Beginning

EHWAZ
Progress

MANNAZ
Acceptance

LAGAZ
Intuition

ING
Accomplishment

DAEG
Vision

OTHEL
Acquisition

Reversed Runes

Runes are either "upright" or reversed. Look at the images of runes on the following pages and you'll see that if you turn them upside down, some of them look very different. These reversed runes have a special meaning in a reading. There are several runes that look the same whichever way they fall.

THE MEANING OF THE RUNES

Fehu

Possessions

The original meaning of this rune was to do with how many cattle you had. The more cattle, the wealthier you were. Nowadays, casting this rune indicates prosperity and material fulfillment in the future, but you will need to work hard to earn that wealth. Share your good fortune with others and make sure you know what your true values are.

Reversed: Frustrated goals. You may be suspicious of others or not be able to work as successfully as you had hoped.

Uruz

Strength

You will soon have the strength and courage to overcome any obstacle. Time to change the circumstances to suit yourself and, with renewed vitality, you will be strong enough to move on from the past. This is a time to welcome change and start to do what you truly want to do.

Reversed: Self-doubt is holding you back. You may meet challenging situations that won't be as hard to overcome as you imagine.

Thurisaz

Challenge

Now is not the time to make hasty decisions, but to take a good look at all the options. Thurisaz warns you not to assume you know all the answers and challenges you to take a step back and resist the temptation to act now. Wait until you have crossed a few more bridges.

Reversed: You regret making a hasty decision, but in the future you will see there is a way to change your mind.

Ansuz

Message

A surprise offer will change your life for the better, or you will encounter someone who may be the signpost to future happiness. Communicating with others will help you to realize a new project, or listen to good advice and learn something to your benefit.

Reversed: Don't trust someone who is only thinking of themselves.

Raidho

Journey

This rune indicates you're about to go on a beneficial trip, whether mental, emotional, or physical. Time to set off in a new direction and explore the world or the bigger picture. Don't fear the unknown. All travel is favored when you cast this rune.

Reversed: You can't decide which direction to take. The signpost isn't helping, so maybe wait until you can see more clearly where the roads ahead lead to.

Kenaz

Clarity

Be honest about your needs, whether sexual or emotional. This rune indicates that you can see more clearly and be truer to your own individual desires. Creative and loving, you will also attract new partners if you're looking for love. A great rune for happy relationships.

Reversed: You will be seduced by a stranger and may resist the attraction. Don't: it will be to your benefit.

Gebo

Relationship

You can now make a commitment and success is guaranteed in any relationship. All kinds of partnerships are favored, even business ones. Gebo reminds you that new romance and seductive strangers will bring you happiness.

Reversed: This rune can't be reversed.

 Fortune Fact

The early rune-makers developed a system of writing from their existing mystical symbols composed of vertical and angled straight lines that could easily be cut or burned into wood.

Wunjo

Success

This is considered the rune of "luck." But don't expect happiness to be handed to you on a plate; you have to make an effort and show your willingness to make changes in your life too. This rune favors creative work, love, children, and professional gain.

Reversed: You don't trust anyone and feel insecure. But the dark clouds will pass away soon.

Hagall

Delay

Whatever plans you have at the moment may be delayed by people or events. This isn't a bad thing, as it will give you time to rethink or modify your ideas or goals. There are challenges ahead, but these are merely stepping stones to your future success. This is a rune of transformation; be ready to go with the flow.

Reversed: This rune can't be reversed.

Nied

Need

As the rune implies, you may be ignoring your needs or adapting too much to other people's demands. When you cast this rune, ask yourself what your real needs are. Don't, however, confuse needs with desires. Think carefully about your emotional and sexual needs for the future.

Reversed: This rune can't be reversed.

Isa

Standstill

This rune indicates you're in limbo, as if time doesn't exist and you can't move forward or back. You're on the threshold of a new cycle in your life, and it will take courage to take that step forward. Pause, reflect, prepare yourself for the journey to come, and then set off into the future.

Reversed: This rune can't be reversed.

Jero

Harvest

Time to cultivate your skills and be confident about reaping the rewards of your efforts. Like any harvest, you must work hard to achieve your best, but in the future there will be plenty of opportunities coming your way. This rune can also indicate that celebrations and rewarding experiences are about to change your life for the better.

Reversed: This rune can't be reversed.

Eihwaz

Action

Make decisive action now. Don't put off the chance to change your life; embrace change rather than resist it. Make what you want clear to someone and make your ideas a reality. With foresight and courage you will gain admiration and transform your image.

Reversed: This rune can't be reversed.

Perth

Secret

Known as the "mystery" rune, this indicates that a secret will be revealed or you're about to discover the truth of a matter. It also tells you that it's time to take charge of your destiny rather than believe your life is fated.

Reversed: Don't live by other people's expectations. Let go of the past, make a choice, and be empowered.

Elhaz

Self-control

Elhaz reminds you that you are about to feel in control of your life. It signifies that you are about to go through a series of fortunate new influences. This could be a new friendship, love affair, or business interest. Don't become too sure of yourself, though; compassion is important when you cast this rune.

Reversed: There are people who could take advantage of your good nature. You are vulnerable, so trust in your intuition and don't listen to unsolicited advice.

Sigel

Vitality

Sigel is known as the rune of success. It indicates that you now have the power to make important changes in your life. You're full of energy, initiative, and confidence, but don't think you can achieve more than you are actually capable of.

Reversed: This rune can't be reversed.

BEHIND THE SIGNS

The Franks Casket

The "Franks Casket" in the British Museum is made of whalebone and exquisitely carved on all surfaces. It dates from the seventh century CE and tells its story in runes, Old English, and Roman script. The front panel shows scenes from the Germanic tale of "Weland the Smith" and the Christian "Adoration of the Magi." The word MAGI is written in runes—Mannaz-Ansuz-Gebo-Isa—just above the three kings.

The Istaby Stone

The Istaby Stone, a memorial stone at Blekinge, is the oldest surviving Danish rune stone. Blekinge, now in Sweden, is an important runic site with four stones that make reference to rune magic and the use of charms. Written on one stone is, "He who breaks these stones will suffer by the hidden forces of rune magic."

Tir

Competition

Indicates you can make rapid progress in your career, and your motivation and competitive spirit will win you success in any endeavor. In love, it can indicate a new romance or positive, exciting feelings, but watch out for rivals.

Reversed: Don't wear your heart on your sleeve. You may lack initiative, so unlock your true potential and fight for what you believe in.

Boerc

Beginning

A sign that something new is about to be born, whether a child, a new you, a love affair, or a creative plan. Nurture your ideas and get cracking. Let go of the past and start afresh. It's time to look ahead and see what you can accomplish if you have patience and self-belief.

Reversed: You know it's time to move on, but you can't free yourself from the past. You must think clearly about what you are so attached to.

Ehwaz

Progress

This rune signifies that all kinds of journeys or adventures are beneficial to you now. You are either about to move home, shift your perspective, or change jobs. You have no choice but to make good progress and influential friends or colleagues will help you to achieve your aims.

Reversed: You are unable to move on for fear of what others think. Make new plans and contacts, and welcome adventure into your life.

Mannaz

Acceptance

Your skills and talents are about to be put to good use, as long as you accept yourself as you are and don't try to be something you're not. It's also time to listen to good advice and communicate your plans to others.

Reversed: You refuse to listen to anyone and people don't seem to understand you. Try being a little more open or tolerant of other people's opinions.

Lagaz

Intuition

Go with the flow of those people who matter to you. The tide is turning in your favor, so trust your intuition too. It's time to move on and not fear change. When you cast Lagaz, it also can mean that an intuitive friend has some great news for you.

Reversed: Concentrate on what needs to be done rather than going off in a dream. Make sure you know what you realistically can do before offering someone help.

Ing

Accomplishment

Something wonderful is about to happen, either a love affair or a new job, or a dream come true. Whatever the case, you can now achieve what you want, and an important opportunity is coming your way. Take time out to enjoy yourself.

Reversed: This rune can't be reversed.

Daeg

Vision

Daeg tells you to believe in yourself and your visions. This is a very positive rune that indicates happiness and long-awaited results. You know the best way to handle any important matters to bring out the best in yourself and others. The sun is shining on you, there's a new day dawning, so make your dreams come true.

Reversed: This rune can't be reversed.

Othel

Acquisition

Financial benefits are coming to you soon. You are about to acquire not only status, but possessions too. But do you really want so much responsibility? Othel asks you to focus carefully on what you want, and more importantly, why.

Reversed: You may be too dependent on material wealth or are about to try to buy yourself out of an emotional situation.

CASTING THE RUNES

HOW TO READ THE RUNIC ORACLES

When you first get your set of runes, lay them all out in their upright positions in front of you. To familiarize yourself with them, pick up one that appeals to you and ask yourself what it may mean to you. Does it make you feel angry, happy, sad? Do you like it, or worry it might mean something negative? Then check the interpretation guide in the previous pages. Always ask positive questions when consulting the runes, just as you did with the Tarot. You can also use the runes as a daily oracle, as described on the page opposite.

A RUNE A DAY

Place the runes in the pouch or bag and shake them gently while you close your eyes and empty your mind. Then, either in your head or out loud, ask the runes to be your guide for the day.

Pick out a single rune from the bag. First think what it might mean, then look at its interpretation.

When you pick a rune, if it's reversed, don't imagine it means something bad. If you look at the brief interpretations of reversed runes, they usually imply that something is lacking in your life, or an issue needs to be explored during the day. As you go about your daily business, observe events, conversations, and experiences in relation to the rune and see how closely it ties in with the energy of the day.

HOW TO CAST THE RUNES

There are many ways to cast the runes. The word "cast" usually means to throw, but it is still used today to refer to the action of scattering a selection of runes onto a prepared table, or drawing runes from a pouch or box to place in a spread or layout.

Here's one casting method, and on the following pages are various spreads you can use with specific placements for interpretation.

1. Either sit at a table, or comfortably cross-legged on the floor.
2. Perform an opening ritual. This can be a moment's meditation, repeating a favorite mantra, or simply closing your eyes and calming your mind as you breathe slowly and deeply.
3. Next, gently shake the bag of runes.
4. Put your hand in the bag and take a rune that "speaks" to you. In other words, when you handle the runes, pick the one that feels right in your hand or between your fingers.
5. Then choose two more runes from the bag, and scatter the three you have chosen in front of you onto the table or floor.
6. Turn any runes that may have fallen symbol-side down face-side up. Now interpret the three runes. The rune closest to you is the current influence, the rune in between is future influences, and the rune farthest away is the outcome.

SIMPLE RUNE SPREAD

This is the simplest form of spread. Use it to discover what's going on in your life right now and how to progress or deal with it to improve your future.

1. Relax and perform your opening ritual.
2. Gently swirl the runes around in the bag with one hand.
3. Select five runes from your bag as you concentrate either on your question, or what needs clarity in your life.
4. As you take each rune, place it in the order shown in the layout below and always place them in the same orientation they were in when you took them from the bag, either upright or reversed.
5. It's quite useful to remember that as you place the runes out, the area on the table or floor represents the world you live in. The runes themselves represent your energies, qualities, and experiences in that world.

1. The issue
2. Helpful influence
3. Challenges
4. Direction
5. Outcome

SAMPLE READING:

You ask how you can improve a static love relationship.

1. **Raidho reversed.** You have too many choices and don't know how to sort it out.
2. **Uruz.** Either your own renewed vitality, or someone who is bold enough to give you good advice.
3. **Mannaz.** Learning to accept help and also realizing what your true desires really are.
4. **Lagaz.** Listen to your heart and give out the love you know intuitively you have to give and you will improve your relationship.
5. **Tir.** Positive results in your love life, and passion returns.

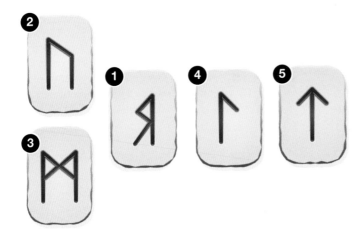

THE CELTIC CROSS

As before, relax and perform your opening ritual, then swirl the runes around in your bag or pouch. You will intuitively know which rune is asking to be picked as you touch them all or run your fingers through them.

This time you're going to pick six runes. Place them out as in the diagram to the right and remember not to turn them upside down if they come out of the bag in the upright position, nor vice versa. Then interpret the runes in relation to your current situation or a specific question.

1. The heart of the matter
2. Challenges
3. Conscious goal
4. Unknown influence
5. Helpful influence
6. Outcome

 Fortune Fact

The Celtic Cross was a common motif in northern Europe. To the Druids, the circle was a symbol of the Moon and feminine energy and the cross a phallic or solar one—the combined symbols creating a fertility motif. It has been suggested that the Celtic Cross was assimilated into Christian symbolism by Saint Patrick in Ireland.

SAMPLE READING:

You want to make a career change.

1. Othel. Financial matters need to be considered.
2. Lagaz reversed. Sort out what you can do in reality, and what you can't.
3. Hagall. You know you want a successful career, and you'll work hard for it.
4. Ing. An unexpected opportunity is coming your way.
5. Perth. Someone will reveal how you can take advantage of the offer.
6. Isa. Be patient; you'll soon be making the change you long for.

NORSE MYTHS AND RUNES

In the *Eddas*, the oldest poem telling the tales of Norse mythology, the god Odin is attributed with discovering runes. To gain wisdom and power of the nine worlds, he pinned himself with his spear to Yggdrasil, the giant ash tree sacred to the gods. According to the ancient scriptures, Odin had to learn nine magical signs and eighteen magical runes to understand the nine realms of existence. The *Eddas* also mentions Bragi, master of the minstrels. Bragi was a great storyteller who reputedly had runes tattooed on his tongue—a reference to his magical gift as a raconteur. Yggdrasil's branches extended up into the heavenly worlds, while three enormous roots extended to the wells of Mimisbrunnr, Urðarbrunnr, and Hvergelmir. The three goddesses known as the Norns lived by the holy well Urðarbrunnr. Each day, they took water from the well and poured it over Yggdrasil so that the branches of the ash wouldn't decay. Beneath the three roots were the realms of Asgard, Jotunheim, and Nifleheim. Four deer ran across the branches of the tree, eating the buds, which represented the four winds. There was also a tree snake and a golden cock that perched on the highest bough. The roots were gnawed by serpents, and on the day of Ragnorak, the end of the universe, the fire giant, Surt, would set the tree on fire.

ODIN'S TREE LAYOUT

Just like Odin hanging from the world tree, you will "hang" your runes in the shape of the tree to discover more about yourself and your future.

As before, select the runes and place them in the layout shown below. This is your world tree.

1. What you need to learn
2. What will challenge you
3. What will guide you
4. The power that will help you
5. What to avoid
6. What to let go of
7. The outcome

SAMPLE READING:

1. **Boerc.** Time to let go of the past and accept that this is a new cycle beginning in your life.
2. **Ansuz.** A surprise offer will make you think twice about what you truly want.
3. **Eihaz.** You will go through a period of new encounters and new love interest or improvement to an old one.
4. **Jero.** Your creative potential and new ideas.
5. **Wunjo.** Don't think that luck is just about chance; you need to put your heart and soul into any new project or love relationship to make it succeed.
6. **Thurisaz.** Let go of the belief that you know all the answers; listen to advice and be objective.
7. **Tir.** This new period in your life will test your spirit of adventure, so be a crusader for your own cause and enjoy living life to the full.

THE I CHING

EASTERN ORIGINS

*T*housands of years ago, Chinese fortune tellers consulted patterns and signs in nature to determine the future. They used the lines and markings on a tortoise's shell, scattered yarrow reeds or coins, and looked at the patterns of flocks of birds in the sky. These methods eventually evolved into an oracle called the **Book of Changes,** or the *I Ching.*

A BRIEF HISTORY OF THE I CHING

The I Ching is based on the symbolism of yin and yang, a mysterious concept that dates back to the early Taoist philosophers, the legendary first emperor of China, Fu Hsi, and the later influential Duke of Zhou. Made up of two opposing energies, for example, dark and light, night and day, or Sun and Moon, they are represented in the I Ching's eight primary trigrams. Based on the belief that nature's basic patterns are a language that reveals everything we do, these eight trigrams represent the fundamental energies of nature.

A trigram is a group of three yin and yang lines in various combinations. Yin, or feminine, lines are broken, and yang, or masculine, lines are unbroken. These are the building blocks of a system that represents the eight energies of the universe. These are: Heaven, Earth, Thunder, Water, Mountain, Wind/Wood, Fire, and Lake.

In the sixth century BCE, the Chinese philosopher and sage Confucius integrated the I Ching into Chinese culture, but it remained relatively unknown until the nineteenth century, when German missionary Richard Wilhelm translated the obscure texts.

At the beginning of the twentieth century, the psychologist Carl Jung saw the I Ching as a confirmation of his own theory of synchronicity. He believed that meaningful coincidences take on a greater significance when more than one occurs simultaneously, such as the throwing of the coins and the oracle's result. This is when the random throwing of the coins connects you to the storehouse of universal knowledge and the revealed oracle gives you insight into your future.

BEHIND THE SIGNS

Yin and Yang

Yin is associated with all things feminine such as the Moon, darkness, intuition, feelings, and right-brain thinking. Yang is associated with all things masculine, such as the Sun, noise, light, action, and left-brain thought processes.

THE EIGHT TRIGRAMS

The eight trigrams represent mysterious Taoist concepts that correspond to the fundamental forces in nature. The interpretations given here are contemporary ones to work with for fortune-telling purposes. You can use these trigrams as a basic oracle to your future by simply looking at them and deciding which one "speaks" to you. Then read its interpretation below.

CHIEN
Heaven
Ancient meaning: The Creative
Color: Gold
Keywords: Achievement, focus, strength
A pure "yang" trigram with three unbroken lines, this trigram represents power, assertiveness, and personal desire. It indicates that you are about to act on your creative ideas and unleash your potential.

Fortune Fact

The origins of the I Ching are also thought to lie with the Duke of Zhou, who lived in the eleventh century BCE. The duke is known as the "God of Dreams," who tells people via their dreams when something important is going to happen to them.

K'UN
Earth
Ancient meaning: The Receptive
Color: Black
Keywords: Receptivity, nurturing, acceptance
The three broken lines are the ultimate symbol of yin, feminine energy. It indicates our need to be loved or nurtured, and what makes us feel secure. This trigram indicates it's time to be patient and accept the flow of events. Things will happen in good time.

CHEN
Thunder
Ancient meaning: The Arousing
Color: Yellow
Keywords: Initiative, spontaneity, insight
This is the trigram of surprises and sudden surprises, just like the first clap of thunder in a storm. It indicates new beginnings and sudden flashes of insight that will bring you success. It's time to use your initiative and get going.

K'AN
Water
Ancient meaning: The Abysmal
Color: Blue
Keywords: Desire, feeling, emotion
Time to trust your instincts and feelings, not fight them. You will need to go with the flow and trust in the energy; don't resist it. Great feelings will soon flow between you and a lover.

KEN

Mountain

Ancient meaning: Keeping Still

Color: Purple

Keywords: Silence, solitude, withdrawal

This trigram indicates you need to take time to reflect before acting. Perhaps spend some time alone and see things from a more objective perspective. There is a need for stillness in your life or for a spiritual awakening.

SUN

Wind/Wood

Ancient meaning: The Gentle

Color: Green

Keywords: Justice, flexibility, fairness

Be fair on yourself, don't judge your actions or feel guilty for them. A time when being fair and adapting to circumstances will improve your life. Compromise will put you in a position of force, not weakness.

LI

Fire

Ancient meaning: The Clinging

Color: Orange

Keywords: Clarity, passion, inspiration

This trigram indicates positive action. Fueled by the power of desire, love, or passion, you will succeed in your goals. Communicate your dreams, cleanse yourself of the past, and all will be clear.

 Fortune Fact

The legendary Fu Hsi reigned in ancient China during the mid-twenty-ninth century BCE. He was a cultural hero said to have invented writing, fishing, and trapping. He discovered the secrets of the I Ching from markings on the back of a mythical dragon horse, or some say a turtle from the Luo River. This discovery is also said to be the origin of calligraphy. He lived for 197 years and died in Chen, now known as Hauiyang, where his monument can still be visited.

TUI

Lake

Ancient meaning: The Joyous

Color: Red

Keywords: Sexual healing, inner calm, secret power

If you choose this trigram, it indicates it's time to get in touch with your inner guide. Within you are all the secrets of the universe, and you have a chance now to access that magic. It's also a time for joy in the world.

HOW TO CONSULT THE I CHING

THE COIN METHOD

*T*he eight trigrams are paired up to make up a total of sixty-four hexagrams. Originally, sixty-four yarrow stalks were cast on the ground to be allocated a hexagram and then interpreted. But this was so complicated that a better system was developed using three coins with distinctive heads and tails.*

You will need: Three coins of the same size with heads and tails, and a pen and paper to draw the hexagram after each throw.

Next, it's important to think of a question or problem in your mind before throwing the coins.

When you are ready, take the three coins and shake them about in your cupped hands. Continue thinking of the issue or question. Then cast them gently onto the table or floor and give value to each side of the coin as follows:

Heads = 3
Tails = 2

Your first throw represents the first line of the hexagram, starting from the bottom. Your second throw represents the next line up, and so on. With six throws you will be creating your hexagram from BOTTOM to TOP.

A total score of 6, 7, 8, or 9 can be obtained with each throw. This results in either a yin or broken line, or a yang or unbroken line.

6 and 8 are **yin** (broken) lines
7 and 9 are **yang** (unbroken) lines

For example, say you threw the following:

1st throw: 2 tails, 1 head, 2 + 2 + 3 = **7**
2nd throw: 2 heads, 1 tail, 3 + 3 + 2 = **8**
3rd throw: 3 heads, 3 + 3 + 3 = **9**
4th throw: 3 tails, 2 + 2 + 2 = **6**
5th throw: 2 tails, 1 head, 2 + 2 + 3 = **7**
6th throw: 3 heads, 3 + 3 + 3 = **9**

After each throw you would write down the number, then write alongside whether it was a yin or yang line.

In this case, you would write from the bottom to the top – 7, 8, 9, 6, 7, 9

This gives the lines starting from the bottom and building up:

Now look at the Table of Hexagrams (p. 124). The left-hand column represents your first three (bottom) throws; the horizontal row, your last three (top) throws. In the example given, the bottom three lines correspond to the trigram Li, and the top three lines to the trigram Sun. The square where they meet gives you the corresponding number of the hexagram (37). Go to pp. 125–131 for its interpretation.

TABLE OF HEXAGRAMS

UPPER ➤ TRIGRAMS LOWER ▼ TRIGRAMS	Ch'ien	Chen	K'an	Ken	K'un	Sun	Li	Tui
Ch'ien	1	34	5	26	11	9	14	43
Chen	25	51	3	27	24	42	21	17
K'an	6	40	29	4	7	59	64	47
Ken	33	62	39	52	15	53	56	31
K'un	12	16	8	23	2	20	35	45
Sun	44	32	48	18	46	57	50	28
Li	13	55	63	22	36	37	30	49
Tui	10	54	60	41	19	61	38	58

INTERPRETING THE HEXAGRAMS

Here is a brief interpretation for the sixty-four hexagrams.

 1. CHI'EN
The Creative
Keyword: Inspiration
Time to take control of your life,
make a dynamic decision,
and move on.

 6. SUNG
Conflict
Keyword: Communicate
Speak up and let someone know your
true feelings. Stay calm and defuse a
clash of wills before it gets complicated.

 2. K'UN
The Receptive
Keyword: Receptive
Be receptive and open to new
ideas. Listen to advice from
someone with experience.

 7. SHIH
The Army
Keyword: Leadership
Provide leadership and support for
your family or colleagues and you will
achieve success.

 3. CHUN
Resolving Difficulties
Keyword: Persevere
Remain calm when all around
you are in chaos. Progress will
be made.

 8. PI
Holding Together
Keyword: Harmony
Be really truthful about your feelings
and you will be rewarded with the
one you love.

 4. MENG
Immaturity
Keyword: Inexperience
Don't get carried away by an impossible
dream. Remember to listen to people
with experience.

 9. HSAIO CH'U
Taming by the Small
Keyword: Humility
Be humble rather than proud and love
will come to you. Don't be put off by
self-doubt.

 5. HSU
Waiting
Keyword: Patience
Remain calm and everything will
work out. A current problem will be
resolved, although maybe not in the
way you expected.

 10. LU
Conduct
Keyword: Simplicity
Keep an open mind, but show that
you are true to your word, and
someone will accept you for who
you are.

11. TAI
Peace
Keyword: Prosperity
A wonderful time for new beginnings.
The feel-good factor is coming your way.

17. SU
Following
Keyword: Acceptance
Welcome change rather than fear it.
It's time to accept your limitations and
those of others.

12. P'I
Standstill
Keyword: Blockage
Circumstances out of your control make
you feel stuck, but now you can modify
your plans. Withdraw from confrontation
and await better times.

18. KU
Removing Corruption
Keyword: Renovation
Show your strength of character
and the doors will open to a
new love affair or career.

13. T'UNG JEN
Fellowship
Keyword: Cooperation
Cooperate and talk things through
with partners. This hexagram indicates
compromise will bring great results.

19. LIN
Approach
Keyword: Advance
Enjoy unexpected opportunities
and a wonderful light shines on your
chosen pathway.

14. TA YU
Possessing Plenty
Keyword: Abundance
A super phase of abundance in love or
personal happiness. Just don't become
arrogant about what you have.

20. KUAN
Contemplation
Keyword: Reflection
Time to reflect carefully on any decision
you have to make.

15. CH'IEN
Modesty
Keyword: Quiet progress
Be modest and people will trust in your
professional ideas and see your talents.

21. SHIH HO
Biting Through
Keyword: Obstacle
Be frank about what you know needs
to be done. Time to persuade others to
change their mindset.

16. YU
Enthusiasm
Keyword: Energy
Any new ideas can now be
communicated. You'll be given a new
opportunity to shine.

22. PI
Grace
Keyword: Beauty
You now have the grace and charm to
attract anyone. Be seductive and enjoy
being flirtatious.

23. PO
Splitting Apart
Keyword: Non-action
Relationships are stormy,
work difficult. But things
that fall apart soon fall
together again.

 24. FU
Return
Keyword: Turning point
Like reaching any threshold,
you're about to step through
into a new period of
exciting change.

 25. WU WANG
Innocence
Keyword: Intuition
The future will unfold the
way you want if you trust in
your intuition. Problems will
soon disappear.

 26. TA CH'U
Taming by the Great
Keyword: Calm
Stay cool and all will be
resolved. A down-to-earth
contact brings you news you've
been waiting for.

 27. I
The Open Mouth
Keyword: Discipline
If you are motivated and
disciplined, you'll be on
the road to great things.
A gossiping colleague could
be a rival.

 28. TA KUO
Preponderance of the Great
Keyword: Pressure
Problems must be resolved, but don't
put yourself under pressure. You may
have to make a small sacrifice to get
things sorted out.

 29. K'AN
The Abysmal
Keyword: Emotion
You know what is right for you, so
don't ignore your feelings. Embrace
change and be emotionally honest
with yourself.

 30. LI
The Clinging
Keyword: Passion
Someone adores your inner fire,
but don't get lost in a cloud of
love; you have your own autonomy
to think about.

 31. HSIEN
Influence
Keyword: Union
This hexagram indicates a love
affair or even a marriage.
A new influence is coming into
your life and you will no longer
be single.

 32. HENG
Duration
Keyword: Stamina
Good fortune comes from integrity
and self-belief. You have all
the powers of persuasion on
your side.

33. TUN
Retreat
Keyword: Withdrawal
Take a long hard look at what you really
want or expect. The time has come to
take a break and think carefully.

 34. TA CHUANG
Power of the Great
Keyword: Empowerment
Be aware of false praise in your
business world, but this is a great time
to influence others and prove your
methods are the right ones.

 35. CHIN
Progress
Keyword: Pathway
This hexagram signifies progress in
whatever you want to achieve. Don't
give up on your own beliefs. Get ready
for an exciting new journey.

 36. MING I
Darkening of the Light
Keyword: Slowing down
Realize that you must reevaluate your
plans and leave a difficult situation.
Time to slow down; good times are
coming your way soon.

 37. CHI JEN
Family
Keyword: Loyalty
Right now, loyalty and respect for your
relationships are needed. Harmony is
indicated if you accept your differences.

 38. K'UEI
Opposition
Keyword: Misunderstanding
Nothing seems fair, and
you're feeling as if everyone is
against you. Let someone close
to you and life will soon be on
your side.

 39. CHIEN
Obstruction
Keyword: Deadlock
You feel as if the world is
against you but the blockage
is all in your mind. In a few
days all will be resolved.

 40. HSIEH
Deliverance
Keyword: Release
Don't brood on past hurts.
It's time to forgive and forget
and soon you will feel as if you
don't have a care in the world.

 Fortune Fact

*Wind is **Feng** and water is **Shui**.
The wind is the active energy, while
water is the passive, yin energy; this
makes up the "ch'i" that flows through
everything. When our homes and
gardens are mapped out according to
the ancient principles of Feng Shui,
the ch'i will flow harmoniously for the
benefit of everyone.*

41. SUN
Decrease
Keyword: Restriction
Don't try too hard to impress, or you will slow down your progress. You must take a cautious approach when dealing with others to achieve what you want.

42. I
Increase
Keyword: Gain
Be creative with your ideas and you will get praise. You will soon be able to show someone special that you have the power to make life good for them too.

43. KUAI
Breakthrough
Keyword: Arrival
This trigram always signifies you will transform your life. You have arrived at a place where you can step across the threshold and make your mark.

44. KOU
Coming to Meet
Keyword: Temptation
Be careful of someone's attitude, style, or seduction of offer. You may be so overwhelmed by what's on offer that you fail to see the truth.

45. TS'UI
Gathering Together
Keyword: Get together
People you know you can trust will be great influences in the near future. Remain focused on your goals and don't let anyone lead you off course.

46. SHENG
Pushing Upward
Keyword: Growth
Welcome new opportunities that will raise your status or personal power. But how a goal is won is more important than the goal.

47. KUN
Oppression
Keyword: Worry
Resist any feelings of doom and gloom and look within for inner strength. In a few days you will have a lovely surprise and wonder why you ever felt down.

48. CHING
The Well
Keyword: Wisdom
Deep within you know the solution to your current problems. Tap the well of knowledge and be enlightened.

49. KO
Revolution
Keyword: Change
Radical change is inevitable, but be responsible for what you need to revolutionize rather than waiting for something to come to you.

50. TING
The Cauldron
Keyword: Nourishment
Nurture your dreams and make them real. You can be assured of success as long as you are honest.

51. CHEN
The Arousing
Keyword: Shock
This hexagram indicates that unpredictable actions may shock other people. Or you may be about to be surprised by events that will, however, be to your benefit.

52. KEN
Keeping Still
Keyword: Stillness
If you keep calm, things will work out the way you want them to. In a few days you will see the answer to a problem with clarity.

Fortune Fact

To the ancient Chinese, Heaven was a universal power. Heaven chose the emperor to rule, yet he was just and fair to the whole world too. If the emperor were evil, Heaven would send natural disasters as a warning. If the emperor failed to listen, Heaven would withdraw its favor and would then choose somebody else to rule.

53. CHIEN
Development
Keyword: Moving
Don't rush into things you might later regret, but it's time to act and make a commitment or seal a deal.

54. KUEI MEI
Marrying Maiden
Keyword: Desire
Romance is out there if you're looking for it, but probably where least expected. You may desire someone who is unavailable.

55. FENG
Abundance
Keyword: Plenty
This is a time to put your trust in your talents and capabilities. With a serious attitude you will achieve your goals.

56. LU
The Wanderer
Keyword: Travel
It's time to travel. All kinds of departures and arrivals are indicated.

57. SUN
The Gentle
Keyword: Consistency
Stick to your beliefs and don't let anyone persuade you otherwise. With persistence you will win great rewards.

58. TUI
The Joyous
Keyword: Fulfillment
Very soon an encounter
with someone will create real
joy and give you the freedom
to be yourself.

59. HUAN
Dispersion
Keyword: Rigidity
A loved one is finding it hard to see
things any other way than their own.
It may be time to tell them gently to
look at life from a new perspective.

60. CHIEH
Limitation
Keyword: Moderation
Time to start saying "no" when you
mean it, rather than saying "yes" just
to get approval or make others happy.

61. CHUNG FU
Inner Truth
Keyword: Acceptance
Lead by example and someone will soon
follow in your footsteps. Do your own thing,
as long as it's generated by inner truth.

62. HSIAO KUO
Preponderance of the Small
Keyword: Non-action
Bide your time, wait for the air to clear,
and don't take risks. Seek advice from
someone wiser who can give you
objective advice.

 Fortune Fact

*To the ancient Chinese, Earth
symbolized everything in nature,
and the world itself was filled
with gods, demons, and spirits.
Legendary dragons roamed the
mountains, and in Feng Shui,
dragon tracks are mapped out in
the landscape to reveal places to
be avoided, or places where it is
beneficial to build a home.*

63. CHI CHI
After Completion
Keyword: Order
Out of chaos usually comes order,
but you need to work at a relationship
issue and harmony will return.

64. WEI CHI
Before Completion
Keyword: Dedication
Times are changing, and if you
dedicate yourself to your mission
or cause, then all will be well and
turn out as you hope.

CHINESE LOVE SIGNS

YOUR LOVE FORECAST AND COMPATIBILITY

*I*n Chinese astrology, apart from animal signs that determine someone's destiny, there are also five elements, known as Fire, Earth, Wood, Metal, and Water. These elements are symbolic of universal energies and how they flow through everything. They are used extensively to map out Feng Shui placements in the home. By knowing your element, you can also discover what kind of love relationships you are likely to have, which are favored, and what kind of love is best for you.

火 **Fire:** Impulsive, passionate, daring

木 **Wood:** Altruistic, independent, freedom-loving

水 **Water:** Romantic, elusive, unpredictable

土 **Earth:** Sensual, possessive, creative

金 **Metal:** Magnetic, powerful, erotic

Just check out the last digit of your year of birth to discover which element you are. If the year of your birth ends with a 1, for example, you are Metal. However, if you were born in January or the first two weeks of February, you may be the previous year's element according to the Chinese lunar calendar. Therefore, check on any good internet site for your correct element.

If you are **yin**, this means you are a gentler version of the element. If you are **yang**, you are a more dynamic version of the element.

YEAR ENDING	ELEMENT
0	Yang Metal
1	Yin Metal
2	Yang Water
3	Yin Water
4	Yang Wood
5	Yin Wood
6	Yang Fire
7	Yin Fire
8	Yang Earth
9	Yin Earth

COMPATIBILITY

	METAL	FIRE	WOOD	WATER	EARTH
METAL	competitive, sexy	torrid, challenging	cool, friendly	confusing, difficult	intense, nurturing
FIRE	torrid, challenging	heated, fun-loving	unpredictable, outrageous	seductive, irresistible	challenging, empowering
WOOD	cool, friendly	unpredictable, outrageous	eccentric, sophisticated	lighthearted, airy	affectionate, careful
WATER	confusing, difficult	seductive, irresistible	lighthearted, airy	playful, romantic	frustrating, provocative
EARTH	intense, nurturing	challenging, empowering	affectionate, careful	frustrating, provocative	intimate, jealous

METAL LOVE SCRIPT

"Magnetic" is a word that partners, lovers, and friends will use about you, and the sparks will fly when you meet potential admirers too. You're fascinated by the power of your own sexuality, but you're independent and find it hard to get truly close to someone. Competitive and ambitious, you may prefer your career to a love relationship. Intimate communication isn't high on your list of priorities, so lovers can often feel you're not there for them. However, when you do meet your match, you are loyal and conventional about your relationship, preferring marriage to living together. If a Fire partner can let you enjoy your autonomy, you can complement each other well. With another Metal partner you may lock swords, but with Earth, the solid, reliable integrity of this element could lead to a highly enriching and sustainable love affair.

 Fortune Fact

FENG SHUI BOOSTER FOR FIRE
Use white candles and silver-edged mirrors to incorporate Metal energy into your home. You could also add black velvet cushions, or silver- or gold-threaded fabrics.

FIRE LOVE SCRIPT

Romance never dies for Fire. Your ideals are huge and your love infectious, and if someone doesn't appear to be the answer to your dreams, you won't stop to ask questions. Impulsively leaping into someone's arms without getting to know them first, you often find yourself in dramatic, yet exciting love affairs. With loads of seductive charm, and an open attitude, you are intent on satisfying your own needs, whether sexual or emotional, and forget your lover has needs too. Water's emotional intensity can put out your spark. Metal may be too driven and controlling, even though sexually dynamic. Wood will tramp across the world as a true fellow spirit and friend. Earth may just offer you enough peace and freedom to do your own thing and be waiting at home for your return.

 Fortune Fact

FENG SHUI BOOSTER FOR METAL
To enhance your sex life, incorporate a little Fire energy into the bedroom, such as red candles, patchouli incense or red bed covers, or place a white quartz crystal beneath your bed.

EARTH LOVE SCRIPT

Harmony, consistency, and security are the most important things for you in love. You are looking for a long-term relationship, where you can feel safe in someone's arms, enjoy a good home life, and commune with nature. On the surface you can appear aloof and serene, but beneath this cool exterior you're intensely passionate in a most seductive way. Very aware of your looks and appearance, you take pride in the person who partners you too, and often fall for good-looking, conventional types. But you can be acutely jealous and possessive, and need to learn to let your partner have their space.

Committed and reliable, the only thing you find difficult in a relationship is taking the odd risk, and you give out so much warmth and affection that you often resent your lover if they don't give it back. Give unconditionally, and nurture that talent. You may enjoy the ever-changing emotions of Water people, but you'll find it hard to accept their unreliable ways. Metal is probably your greatest affinity and will complement your own strengths. However, Fire has the insight to know what you truly desire.

Fortune Fact

FENG SHUI BOOSTER FOR EARTH
Earth needs to bring the energy of Water into your home, such as images of waterfalls, oceans, rivers, rain, or a group of shells in a bowl on your window ledge.

WOOD LOVE SCRIPT

Gregarious and free-spirited, you often go out of your way to avoid making a commitment that might compromise you. Even though you can talk your way in and out of any debate, you aren't keen on communicating your physical and emotional needs. Preferring an unconventional love life, you want a lighthearted, fun-loving time and avoid long intimate chats and slushy sentiments. Sexy and carefree, all you want is to be given space to be yourself, and your ideal partner is someone who has that outlook on life too. Your seductive skills are classy, and you admire perfection and experimentation in a partner.

You get on well with Fire, but as lovers they are often too demanding and proud, while Earth is too possessive. Metal's conventional needs may clash with your more radical ones. With Water you'll discover romance and the space you need. But perhaps only another Wood partner can really understand your freedom-loving lifestyle and be your perfect match.

 Fortune Fact

FENG SHUI BOOSTER FOR WOOD

Place rose quartz on your bedside table or window ledge to promote Earth energy. Also incorporate ochers and rich umber colors into your soft furnishings, or hang a tapestry or antique painting on your wall.

Fortune Fact

FENG SHUI BOOSTER FOR WATER
To enhance your love life, bring Wood elements into your bedroom, such as soft green fabrics, wooden sculptures, or a piece of gnarled driftwood placed on your window ledge, and also a carnelian crystal to promote happiness.

WATER LOVE SCRIPT

Romance is high on your agenda, and when you fall in love, you fall hard. Yet you do find it easy to fall for a complete stranger when you're already partnered with someone else. Your feelings change with the wind, so it's hard for you to know what you really feel. Being so sensitive to other people's moods, you often play the role that someone else wants you to play and never really get to be the real you. Somehow you are the ultimate paradox: inconsistent, but in need of a permanent lover; unpredictable, but still there for someone if you are in love. Sustaining a relationship is hard for you unless you get an awful lot of variety from one person. You often believe that what you haven't got is what you truly want, and what you have got is what you don't really need. Earth will frustrate you with their possessive ways. Metal will be intensely attracted to you, but their need for reliability will cause great tension. Fire is sexually delightful, but can play too many games with your heart. Wood, more than any other element, will keep you longing for more of their extrovert ways.

THE SECRET LANGUAGE OF CRYSTALS

HOW CRYSTALS REVEAL YOUR FUTURE

Crystals are concentrated electromagnetic energy fields of light. Used as adornments throughout history, gemstones and crystals invoke powerful healing energies and have long been employed as divinatory tools. They can be laid out in a spread like the tarot cards and runes. Alternatively, one can be picked from a pouch or bag as your crystal guide or oracle for the day. Events and encounters throughout the day will align with the symbolic language of the crystal and empower you with its specific qualities. For example, say you randomly choose aquamarine, the chances are you will have a flirtatious or romantic encounter.

SCIENCE

All crystals and gemstones vibrate to what is known as the piezoelectric effect, discovered by French physicist and chemist, Pierre Curie (1859–1906). When squeezed or stretched, a voltage is produced across the crystal's face. This effect is reversible, and if the polarity of the voltage is alternated, the crystal will rapidly expand and contract, producing a vibration. This is the key to how quartz watches function.

CRYSTALS AND THE ZODIAC

As long ago as 4000 BCE, the ancient Mesopotamians used astrology and the stars to predict the future. They also thought that rock crystals were linked to planets and their energy, which reflected the cosmos and its vibrations. The ancient Greeks believed that every piece of clear quartz crystal is a fragment of the Universal Crystal of Truth. Crystals correspond to the twelve signs of the zodiac and the planets, and each crystal vibrates to the astrological resonance of the planets and the signs.

CHOOSING CRYSTALS

Ideally you should choose one each of the twelve zodiac crystals and the ten planetary crystals. If you can't get hold of them, then you can always replace them with other crystals associated with the zodiac signs and planets. Most New Age stores will have them clearly marked. It doesn't matter if they are polished or not, as long as they are similar in size and shape, so that when you pick one from the bag you can't tell which is which.

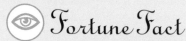

Fortune Fact

When you are selecting a crystal to buy, hold each one in your hand until you know it's the right one for you, even for thirty seconds. Sometimes you will feel a vibrational energy, or have an intuitive flash. This is a sign that you're in tune with the vibrational energy of the crystal and the cosmos's divining power.

CRYSTAL ORACLES

In ancient Greece, fortune telling was performed by seers who not only looked at the patterns of flocks of birds in flight, or the ripples in a pool, they also cast crystals to predict the future. Oracles were people through whom the gods spoke or gave messages directly to the individual. Shrines and temples were set up for the gods specifically so they could send their messages through the temple priests. The most important oracles of Greek antiquity were Pythia, priestess to sun-god Apollo at Delphi, and Dodona, oracle of Dione and Zeus.

In the sixth century BCE, Tarquinius, the last king of Rome, bought the Sibylline Books from the Cumaean Sibyl, the priestess of the Apollonian oracle at Cumae, near Naples. This collection of oracular utterances was consulted at key moments in the history of the Roman Empire and Republic.

BEHIND THE SIGNS

Chakras and Crystals

Eastern spiritual traditions maintain that universal energy, known as "prana" in India, and "ch'i" in Chinese philosophy, flows through the body linked by seven subtle energy centers known as chakras. The word "chakra" is a Sanskrit word meaning "wheel." These energies constantly revolve or spiral around and through our bodies vibrating at different frequencies, in an upward vertical direction. Specific crystals respond to the electromagnetic charge that is coursing through our bodies. If our chakral energy is under-active, the corresponding vibration of the stones will help to harmonize, balance, and stimulate these energies. If overactive, certain stones will help to subdue the energy.

THE TEN PLANETARY CRYSTALS OF SUCCESS

By wearing or carrying a specific crystal you can direct your own future toward personal success. Here are the ten crystals that correspond to the ten planetary energies. Depending on the attributes of the crystal, choose the one that can give you the kind of success you're looking for and place it on your desk at work or home.

URANUS • Orange carnelian

Promotes progressive thinking. Helps you break free from conventional ideas or habits.

VENUS • Tourmaline

Attracts people to you. Carry this when you're looking for new romance.

NEPTUNE • Blue lace agate

Gives great clarity. Wear this to promote great visions and life-changing contacts.

SATURN • Onyx

Carry or wear this to bring you material gain and new values. Financial reward can also be expected.

JUPITER • Lapis lazuli

Known as the "eye of wisdom," promotes career success and new insight.

MARS • Red agate

Gives you a shot of courage and powerful initiative, and helps you prove a point.

MERCURY • Topaz

Assists decision-making, good for traveling, and great for communicating ideas.

THE MOON • Opal

Gets you more in touch with what others are feeling or thinking. Makes you more aware of your own desires.

THE SUN • Clear quartz

The action crystal. Carry this and you'll get things done and start new projects.

PLUTO • Amethyst

A passionate relationship will be beneficial and transform your life.

THE TWELVE ZODIAC CRYSTALS

There are in total twenty-two zodiac crystals, which also correspond to the twenty-two Major Arcana cards of the zodiac. However, if you manage to get just the twelve zodiac sign crystals and not the remaining ten planetary crystals, you can work with these for now. For good luck in the future, wear or carry your own zodiac sign crystal. Here is a brief guide to what the twelve zodiac crystals can bring you.

ARIES • **Red carnelian**
Brings adventure, inventive friends, and beneficial challenges.

TAURUS • **Rose quartz**
Helps you to improve relationships or to meet the perfect partner.

GEMINI • **Citrine**
Travel is favored; quick decisions can be made successfully.

CANCER • **Moonstone**
Trust in your intuition; emotional strength will win through.

LEO • **Tiger's eye**
Dare to be different or dramatic in love; indicates a fiery admirer.

VIRGO • **Peridot**
You can make a serious choice; work opportunities beckon.

LIBRA • **Jade**
A seductive stranger takes you by surprise; indecision about love.

SCORPIO • **Malachite**
Resolution of money issues; success in joint affairs.

SAGITTARIUS • **Turquoise**
Travel imminent; love is boundless.

CAPRICORN • **Obsidian**
Changes for the better; professional success or job promotion.

AQUARIUS • **Amber**
Radical ideas will work; be open-minded to new ideas.

PISCES • **Aquamarine**
Romance is in the air; a little dream can come true.

HOW TO CONSULT THE CRYSTALS

The first method for consulting the crystals is simply to place all your crystals in a pouch or bag. If you can, try to include a piece of clear quartz crystal to represent clarity, and a piece of amethyst for beneficial change. If you choose these in the spread on p. 148, then they are doubly important for you.

1. Sit quietly and close your eyes. Focus on a question or issue, such as "Will new romance come my way?"
2. Put your hand inside the pouch and take your first piece of crystal. As you feel inside, just like with the runes, handle the crystals gently until you feel as if one is speaking to you.
3. Place the crystal on the table or floor in front of you. This is the Crystal of Light, representing your current self, and the energy you are radiating to the world.
4. Take another crystal. This is the Crystal of Shadows, representing outside influences, people, or blockages.
5. The third crystal is the Crystal of Fortune, which represents the future outcome of your question.

Use the brief keywords and the following interpretations to help you. For example, let's say you choose citrine as the Crystal of Light, red carnelian as the Crystal of Shadows, and amber as the Crystal of Fortune. The answer to whether love is coming your way would be:

Citrine. Your current communication talents will help you find romance.
Red carnelian. Pushy friends may think they know what's best for you.
Amber. An unusual or unexpected encounter will bring you the kind of person you're looking for.

CRYSTAL INTERPRETATIONS

Here are interpretations for all twenty-two crystals. Always widen your interpretation to relate to the question you've asked. Intuition is an invaluable tool for telling someone's fortune because it means that you're connecting to a psychic language, rather than just relying on the words on a page. The crystal's vibrational energy will help you to draw on your own psychic ability and it is that psychic sense that reads and listens to the language coming from the universal storehouse of knowledge.

RED CARNELIAN

Keyword: Activate
Oracle: You can achieve whatever you want now, as long as you conquer any fears or self-doubt. Start making headway with your plans and your drive for success will pay off.

ROSE QUARTZ

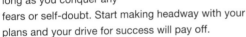

Keyword: Love
Oracle: There is a chance for a wonderful rapport between you and someone special, or a love match is well favored. If single, you're about to meet someone who will change your life. All relationships can now improve.

CITRINE

Keyword: Communicate
Oracle: This crystal enables you to transform negative thoughts into positive ones. You are about to make a good decision based on logic, and communication and all forms of travel are beneficial.

MOONSTONE

Keyword: Belonging
Oracle: Your intuition and feelings are powerful, and it's time to go with what your heart truly wants. Take care you aren't being deceived by those who want to manipulate you. Family values may need reevaluating.

TIGER'S EYE

Keyword: Inspire
Oracle: A time when any new quest can be successfully completed, and a time to be different and show you have purpose and vision. Love relationships will be dramatic and challenging.

PERIDOT

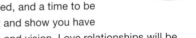

Keyword: Discriminate
Oracle: It's time to make decisions based on all the facts. Discriminate with care and make sure you have all the evidence before making any decision. It's also time to spread your wings and interact with people who respect your individuality.

JADE

Keyword: Harmony
Oracle: This crystal indicates a harmonious love life and success in romance. You are in harmony with the universe, so manifest your desires, just take care you're not blind to the truth of someone's feelings for you.

MALACHITE

Keyword: Transform

Oracle: This crystal is often known as the "sleep stone" because of its hypnotic effect. This stone also indicates that

you can transform your life as long as you stay awake to opportunity. Material success is also coming your way.

TURQUOISE

Keyword: Travel

Oracle: Journeys are indicated, whether physical or intellectual. Explore new ideas, feel free of obligations, and you can now live

life to the full. Love is boundless and you'll soon be free of past regrets.

OBSIDIAN

Keyword: Materialize

Oracle: The stone of manifestation. You can now ground your goals and improve all aspects of your lifestyle. If you have a vision, turn it now

into a reality. Persevere, and any challenges will be rewarded with a wonderful run of events.

AMBER

Keyword: Rationalize

Oracle: You have some radical plans and rebellious friends, but somehow you know that unconventional methods are

going to work in your favor. Don't give up on fighting for your beliefs. They're the right ones.

AQUAMARINE

Keyword: Romance

Oracle: A stone of harmony and love. There will shortly be romance in the air, and the tide is turning in your favor. Don't

let other people's negativity stop you from doing what's best for you.

CLEAR QUARTZ CRYSTAL

Keyword: Clarity

Oracle: Your life will soon be filled with joy and a sense of personal success. You can now see clearly where you are

going and why. Any difficult situations will soon be resolved and the air cleared.

OPAL

Keyword: Sensitivity

Oracle: You're acutely sensitive to other people's wishes, and feelings may be running high. Concentrate on your own beliefs

and values and remember you can't change things that cannot be changed.

TOPAZ

Keyword: Understanding

Oracle: You can now make the right decision and follow it through with excellent results. Be more tolerant of other people and less judgmental

and it will bring you the results you're looking for. If someone is making you feel invisible, don't let them.

TOURMALINE

Keyword: Compassion

Oracle: Friends are important to you now and can give you good, objective advice. You will soon find true love if you respect your own needs; or, a lover is now ready to commit.

RED AGATE

Keyword: Initiative

Oracle: You can make progress in any work or relationship issue and resolve all problems. You must make it clear what you want, and why. A stranger brings unexpected but welcome ideas.

LAPIS LAZULI

Keyword: Wisdom

Oracle: The eye of wisdom indicates that you must use your head and not your heart. You can now forge ahead with career matters, educate yourself in new ideas, and widen your perspective. A global viewpoint will bring you success.

ONYX

Keyword: Structure

Oracle: Onyx indicates that organization, structure, and consistency are important qualities in your life now. You need a reliable set of rules to live by, and you feel in control of your life. But don't let material wealth matter to you, or someone else, more than love.

ORANGE CARNELIAN

Keyword: Rebellion

Oracle: Be innovative and promote some positive life changes. People may frustrate you but press ahead with your plans. Lovers may be radical, or refuse to play the game your way.

BLUE LACE AGATE

Keyword: Vision

Oracle: With imagination and vision, worldly success can be yours. Your idea can be made manifest, but don't sacrifice it for the sake of someone else.

AMETHYST

Keyword: Passion

Oracle: A passionate love affair is indicated, or it's time to end one relationship and begin another. Time to transform your world.

 ⊙ *Fortune Fact*

Lapis lazuli is a rare stone, used by the ancient Egyptians in magical amulets and scarab rings. Cleopatra used powdered lapis for eyeshadow.

CRYSTAL SPREADS

Here are two different spreads to try out. You can also invent your own, or use the tarot layout examples in this book to guide you.

1. The best place to read crystals is actually out in the open—on a beach, in a garden or park, or some other natural space. The time of year can be important too, and readings during the waxing crescent moon cycle, as well as the summer solstice and spring equinox, will enhance your fortune-telling powers.
2. If you do read your crystal spread indoors, place a cloth or silk scarf on the table or floor first, to enhance the vibrational quality of the stones.
3. Start your ritual either by lighting a candle or incense, or using a meditation technique. If you are outside, cast an imaginary circle of protection around you by pointing your finger in a circle as you turn 360 degrees. First, cast the circle clockwise, then counterclockwise. This will protect you and your crystals and harmonize your own energy with that of the universe.

IN THE FUTURE SPREAD

Pick a total of five crystals from your pouch and lay them out in the order shown below.

1. Your current mood
2. Your future desire
3. Good influence
4. Difficult influence
5. The outcome

SAMPLE READING:

1. **Turquoise.** You're restless and feeling quite irresponsible.
2. **Amethyst.** You long for a passionate love affair.
3. **Lapis lazuli.** If you widen your network or study a new subject, you'll meet up with the right kind of potential lovers.
4. **Malachite.** Don't let materialistic or financial needs cloud your judgment.
5. **Tourmaline.** An easygoing admirer will soon be charming you out of your restless mood.

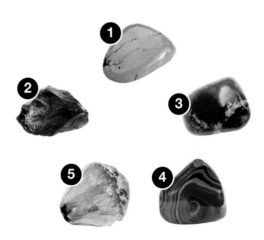

COMPATIBILITY SPREAD

This is a useful spread to see how compatible you are with someone, whether a new friend, work colleague, or lover.

1. My current self
2. The other person
3. Together now
4. Our mutual test
5. Our destiny together

As before, take five crystals one at a time from your pouch and lay them out in the order shown.

SAMPLE READING:

You've just met someone you see as a potential lover. Will it be a match made in heaven?
1. Red carnelian. I'm feeling dynamic and full of spirit.
2. Jade. They are romantic and at one with the universe.
3. Moonstone. Feelings strong for each other.
4. Topaz. Be tolerant of each other's differences.
5. Red agate. Progressive, if you both enjoy crusading for a mutual cause.

BEHIND THE SIGNS

Good Omens

Crystals were used to protect and attract good omens by Babylonian astrologers as they gazed at the stars. At night, they placed crystals on the ground in alignment with the most important constellation of the season. They would look into the crystals and those that shone the brightest or refracted glowing prisms of color would be worn on the body to protect and encourage beneficial energy from the planetary forces.

PENDULUM DOWSING

USING A PENDULUM FOR FORTUNE TELLING

The art of dowsing is recorded as far back as ancient Egypt, where pendulums were used to decide the best place to grow crops. Romans were condemned for using pendulums to plot against the Emperor Caligula. In the first century CE, Roman scholar Mercellinus showed how a heavy ring hanging on a thread was swung around the circumference of a circle. The circle was marked out with the alphabet and as the pendulum swung, it spelt out answers to questions. Traditionally, a pendulum is used to dowse the sex of an unborn child.

In ancient Greece, priestesses held out a forked piece of wood to interpret prophecies transmitted through the vibrational forces of the gods. Dowsing was once known as "water-witching" and the word identified with the old English "*dewsys*" (goddess) and "*rhodi*" (tree branch), but it is more commonly thought to originate in a Middle German word, "*duschen*," to strike.

In the early nineteenth century, an Italian scientist, Francesco Campetti, used a dowsing rod to discover water and minerals underground. Most dowsing rods were made of tree branches indigenous to the area, such as hazel and willow, which are particularly supple and bend easily.

There are two main forms of dowsing. The most well known is the use of rods to discover underground water, metals, and oil. The other is the use of a pendulum, usually made of crystal or polished metal, to find lost objects, make decisions, and look into the future. You can use a pendulum to reveal your own inner desires, answer important questions, and even to select a potential partner.

HOW DOES DOWSING WORK?

Dowsing rods and pendulums are thought to be a bridge between the vibrational forces of the universe and the diviner. The diviner, or dowser, interprets the messages sent from the cosmos. It is also believed that some people have an innate sensitivity to changes in the magnetic field, particularly when finding water or lost objects. Cosmic energy permeates your unconscious mind, and so the muscles of your hand holding the pendulum react without you realizing it. This is called the "ideomotor response." Tiny involuntary movements of the muscles cause the pendulum to move and are amplified by the pendulum.

BEHIND THE SIGNS

Perfect Pendulum

There are many different types of pendulum available these days. Crystal ones are particularly attractive and have their own vibrational energy too. Opt for the one you like because of its look, but also its weight when you dangle it between thumb and forefinger. Round, cylindrical, or spherical shapes are best because they swing more accurately. There are four main types of pendulum: the pyramid, the cylinder, the faceted crystal, and the Mermet. The Mermet has a top that unscrews to reveal a cavity in which to place a sample of what you're looking for. Of course, you can always make your own pendulum by hanging a heavy ring on a piece of fine thread.

ASKING QUESTIONS

There are certain points to remember when asking questions. You can ask the pendulum virtually anything, but remember: you will only have four possible answers. These are, "Yes," "No," "I don't know," and "Ask again." So the way you ask the question is just as important as the answer.

There's no point asking a question that gives a choice. For example, "Should I go to Spain or Italy for my holiday?" Nor is there any point asking a question that demands information, such as "How can I make X fall in love with me?"
So you could ask, "Is it a good idea to go to Spain for my holiday?"
"Will X fall in love with me?"
"Will it be sunny on Monday?"

You can also locate items. To do this, you will have to go to various locations throughout the room or house, and at each spot ask, "Is the object here?" All these questions have possible yes/no answers.

STEP-BY-STEP GUIDE

1. Begin by sitting at a table and resting your elbow lightly on it. Alternatively, stand with your arm extended over the place you wish to dowse.

2. Hold the end of the thread, or chain, of your pendulum between your thumb and first finger, using very little pressure, in a relaxed way. The pendulum should be hanging about 12 inches (30 centimeters) in front of you.

3. Make sure that your elbow is the only point of contact with the table. If you are standing, bend your arm at an angle of 90 degrees so that your forearm is parallel with the ground. Make sure your legs and feet are uncrossed, as this blocks the energy flow.

4. Swing the pendulum gently to get used to the feel of it. Experiment to see whether a longer or shorter "drop" works best for you. Once you feel comfortable with the drop, grab the pendulum with your other hand to stop the movement.

5. Make sure that your body is relaxed and your mind still. If you have never used a pendulum before, it can take a while before any movements start, so be patient for its response. The pendulum may just move very slightly at first, but after a while it can build up quite considerable movement. Remember, this is triggered by the vibrational forces of the universe affecting the tiny muscles in your arms and hand. The pendulum will work better if you remain open and imaginative and trust in the universe and the energies flowing through you.

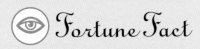

Fortune Fact

Your pendulum will move in one of four ways:

1. A clockwise swing
2. A counterclockwise swing
3. A side-to-side swing
4. An up-and-down swing

SWINGS AND ROUNDABOUTS

Now find out which swing is which for you. The swings are not the same for everyone; some people find the clockwise is a "yes" and the counterclockwise is a "no," or vice versa.

First, ask a question to which you know the answer. For example: "Am I female?" (If you're female then it will answer "yes." Obviously, if you're male, you would ask, "Am I male?")

Whichever way the pendulum swings gives you your "yes" swing.

Now ask a question to which you know the answer is "no" to get your "no" swing.

Now ask a question to which the answer will be "don't know"; for example, a silly question like, "Are there two coins in my friend's pocket?" gets your "don't know" swing. The remaining swing will be the "ask again" swing.

Make a note of each swing; these responses will remain the same for every time you use the pendulum. If you do stop using the pendulum for a long period of time, then check again as your energy responses may have changed.

Finally, once you've established the four swings, you can now ask the pendulum questions to which you REALLY don't know the answers. This is when your unconscious starts to connect to the universal energy and generates the pendulum's response. Have fun asking questions, and be positive. But take care you don't project your own desires into the movement of the pendulum.

EXERCISE TO DEVELOP YOUR ABILITIES

We often unconsciously take control of the pendulum swings, and it is this power that can lead to wrong answers, or projected outcomes of our own desires. So it's important to learn to "let go" of your mind while dowsing. Here's how:

1. Suspend the pendulum until it's motionless.

2. Out loud or in your head, tell the pendulum to move in a clockwise direction. Do not move your arm, wrist, or hand.

3. Concentrate on the pendulum by staring at it, and thinking or saying, "clockwise, clockwise," over and over again until the pendulum starts to move in that direction.

4. Stop the pendulum, then think hard about another direction, and you will find it again follows your thoughts.

5. Now free yourself from the power of your conscious mind by focusing on the pendulum but don't think about it. If you can't "think of nothing" then repeat your chosen question like a mantra in your head, so that you are still receptive to the power of the universe. With practice, you'll learn to know the difference between intentionally causing the pendulum to move and a genuine response.

BEHIND THE SIGNS

Lost Objects

Pendulums are often used to find lost objects. Practice by getting someone to hide an object such as a key in one specific room. Ask obvious questions like, "Is the key in this room?" to check that the pendulum is working for you. Ask precise questions, like, "Is the key under the mat?" or "Is the key in the drawer of the table?" and so on. Soon, the pendulum will respond positively over the correct place.

BEHIND THE SIGNS

Be Honest

When predicting the future, we are all highly subjective and tend to project our unconscious desires and wishes onto the outcome. We are capable of controlling the swing of the pendulum to fit with what we would like to happen. So this means you have to be really honest when using the pendulum to find out things about yourself.

PREDICTING THE FUTURE

Try out this card test to establish your level of objectivity.

1. Take four playing cards and shuffle them.
2. Take the top card and look at it. This is going to be the card that your pendulum has to "find" or predict where it is. Say you choose the ten of clubs.
3. Mix and shuffle the four cards again, face-down, until you really and honestly don't know where the ten of clubs is.
4. Place them face down in a row in front of you.
5. Ask the pendulum to find the card. Suspend it over each card in turn and ask, "Is this the ten of clubs?" Be patient if it takes a while to move.
6. The pendulum should give you a "no" for three cards and a "yes" for the right one. If it's wrong, you still need to practice letting go of your conscious control. Practice eventually makes perfect.
7. Whether you're about to change your lifestyle, go for a job interview, or start a new relationship, write your question down on a piece of paper and suspend the pendulum over the question.

For example, a very simple question would be, "Will I get the job?" Always ask specific questions, and again always relax, quieten your mind, and close your eyes so you can't see which way the pendulum is moving. Sometimes this helps to give a more objective influence to your pendulum fortune telling.

TESTING A RELATIONSHIP

To discover if you will have a harmonious relationship with someone, try out the following pendulum test.

1. Select two coins of the same size and value. Place them on a table a little way apart, then suspend your pendulum between the two coins. Your pendulum should swing in a positive way, as the two coins are obviously the same and in harmony in substance, shape, and value.

2. Next, replace one of the coins with something like a pen, card, or ring. Suspend the pendulum again between the two items, and this time you may get a negative response, or the pendulum might not move at all. This means they are not in harmony.

3. You can now apply this method to two "people." Say you're about to go on a date and wonder how you might get on. Write your names on two small pieces of paper, the same size, then place them on the table about 5 inches (13 centimeters) apart and suspend the pendulum between them. Again, if you get a positive response, you will get on well with each other; if it's negative, it may mean you're not meant for each other; a "don't know" could mean that you are going to find it hard to get close; and a "try again" means maybe you need to go on more than one date to find out!

TEA LEAF READING

HOW TO READ TEA LEAVES

Known as **tasseomancy,** interpreting the patterns of tea leaves, coffee grounds, and even wine sediment has been a long-held tradition in many cultures. The word derives from the French word for cup, "tasse," from the Arabic "tassa," and from "manteia," an ancient Greek word for divination. Western tasseomancy can be traced to medieval European fortune tellers who first predicted the future by reading the patterns in nature and the way wax falls from a candle. When Dutch merchants introduced tea from China into Europe in the seventeenth century, tea leaf reading evolved and became highly popular. Included here is a varied list of the most basic meanings of the common shapes seen in the teacup.

TEA LEAF READING RITUAL

Tea leaf reading involves not just the reading of the patterns, but the whole ritual of drinking and enjoying your tea to get you in a relaxed state of mind. If you don't like tea, you can use coffee that has coffee grounds in it, such as Turkish or Greek-style coffee, or just sprinkle some fresh grounds into the remaining liquid after you have drunk it.

For tea, you need to make it the old-fashioned way in a teapot. Use a teacup with a wide mouth and sloping sides and loose tea with small- to medium-sized leaves. The cup must be undecorated on the inside so you can see the patterns made by the tea leaves clearly. Let the tea brew for several minutes, then pour the tea into your cup without straining it. Let the leaves settle in the bottom, then as you drink your tea think of the questions or issues that are on your mind for the future. It's often more fun to do tea leaf reading with friends so you can all peer into your cups and read each other's tea.

When there is barely any liquid left in the cup, but enough to swish the leaves around, take the cup and swirl the tea leaves around three times in a counterclockwise direction, then cover the cup with the saucer, invert the cup and saucer, and allow the liquid to drain off into the saucer. Then pick up the cup and see what shapes and patterns have emerged.

If you are using coffee, do the same thing. In many Middle Eastern cultures, the drinker "opens the heart" by placing the right thumb on the inside bottom of the cup and twisting clockwise slightly. The impression that is left by this small action is interpreted as the drinker's feelings.

BEHIND THE SIGNS

Early Signs

Before you even start the reading, there may be some early signs to interpret:

- **Bubbles on the surface of the tea means that money is on its way.**
- **If any tea leaves are floating on the surface, then expect visitors. The number of leaves shows how many days away they are.**
- **If two teaspoons are accidently placed on a saucer, then you can expect news of twins!**

READING THE LEAVES

Most tea leaf readers consider the patterns nearest the rim to be concerned with the immediate future, while those at the bottom of the cup are the distant future. So if you had asked, "When will I get news of my job interview?" any leaves near the rim indicate you'll hear about it within twenty-four hours, whilst any at the bottom mean you will hear in a few days.

To read the leaves, hold the cup so that the handle is pointing toward you, the questioner. If you are reading for someone else, make sure the handle is pointing toward them. The handle represents the questioner, and the tea leaves are read in relation to the position of the handle.

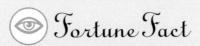

Fortune Fact

Romany "gypsies" known for their fortune-telling skills helped to spread tea leaf reading around Europe in the nineteenth century. It became very popular throughout the British Isles during Victorian times, mostly as a parlor game for amusement.

Leaves that are arranged to the right of the handle indicate the future, and leaves to the left of the handle indicate the past. The farther away the leaves lie from the handle, the further away the events are in time or physical distance.

There may be some very obvious signs that speak to you.

For example, if there are still some drops of liquid that have remained in the cup, they may represent tears or unhappiness.

A very large clump of leaves with no distinct pattern means that there are problems in your life that have not been resolved. If the leaves are near the handle, this is through your own decisions; if they are far away from the handle, it's not your fault, but you may have to instigate some changes.

The symbols at the base of the cup also refer to emotions and deeper unconscious desires; those nearer the rim refer to day-to-day ordinary experiences. The bigger the symbol, the more importance it will have in your life. The area near the handle represents home and family. Symbolic images of strangers are usually at the opposite side of the cup, and lovers to the right.

On the following pages is an alphabetised list of example patterns or shapes you might see, and their most simple meaning. With practice, you will begin to see the shapes, intuit their meanings, and put together a story of the future revealed by the patterns in the cup.

BEHIND THE SIGNS

Fortune-telling Cups

These days there is a whole range of cups specially designed for tea leaf reading, such as zodiac cups that contain planetary and astrological symbols. The placement of these symbols encourages the reader to combine astrology with the patterns formed by the leaves. There are also cups that show tiny images of playing cards, and one-word interpretations on the cards. Finally, there are cups decorated with tiny symbols that are interpreted in a booklet for easy reference. The symbols appear both on the inside and outside of the cups, and on the saucers.

Two rings

INTERPRETING THE LEAVES

Acorn: Success. Top of cup—financial success.

Angel: Good news.

Basket: If empty—money worries.
  If full—a present.

Bee: Good news.
  Near handle of cup—friends gathering.
  Swarm of bees—success with an audience.

Bell: Unexpected news.
  Near top of cup—promotion.
  Two bells—joy. Several bells—a wedding.

Bird: Good news, opportunities.

Book: Open—expect legal actions,
  future success.
  Closed—delays, difficult studies.

Bouquet: Love and happiness.

Box: Open—romantic troubles solved.
  Closed—finding something.

Bracelet: Impending marriage.

Cage: A proposal.

Cat: A quarrel, treachery, a false friend.

Chimney: Hidden risks.

Crescent: A journey.

Dove: Good fortune.

Eagle: A change for the better.

Egg: Prosperity, success—the more eggs the better.

Fairy: Joy and enchantment.

Feather: Instability, lack of concentration.

Fish: Good fortune in all things.

Fork: A false friend, flattery.

Gate: Opportunity, future happiness.

Hat: A new occupation, a change.
  In bottom of cup—a rival.
  At side of cup—diplomacy.

Feather

Swarm of bees

Heart: Love and marriage, a trustworthy friend.

Initials: People you know—useful contacts.
　　Unknown initials—strangers will be useful.

Key: New opportunities, doors opening.
　　Crossed keys—success.

Ladder: Promotion.

Leaf: Prosperity.

Lines: Straight and clear—progress, journeys.
　　Wavy—uncertainty.
　　Slanting—business problem.

Man: Near handle of cup—a visitor.
　　Clear and distinct—dark-haired visitor.
　　Not well-defined—fair-haired visitor.
　　With arm outstretched—bearing gifts.

Necklace: Complete—admirers.
　　Broken—the end of a relationship.

Palm tree: Happiness in love.

Parasol: A new lover.

Parcel: A surprise.

Question mark: Hesitancy, caution.

Rainbow: Happiness, prosperity.

Ring: Near top of cup—marriage.
　　Near middle of cup—proposal.
　　Near bottom of cup—long engagement.
　　Complete ring—happy marriage.
　　Broken ring—broken engagement.
　　Two rings—plans working out.

Shell: Good news.

Ship: Successful journey.

Square: A symbol of protection, comfort, peace.

Swallow: Decisiveness, unexpected journeys.

Sword: Disappointment, quarrels.

Tree: Changes for the better, ambitions fulfilled.

Umbrella: Annoyances, a need for shelter.

Vase: A friend in need.

Wasp: Trouble in love.

Waterfall: Prosperity.

Weather vane: Indecisiveness ahead.

Wheel: Complete—good fortune.
　　Broken—disappointment.
　　Near rim of cup—unexpected money.

Wings: Many messages.

Woman: Pleasurable event.

GEOMANCY

FORTUNE TELLING WITH MAGIC ORACLES

ranslated from ancient Greek, geomancy literally means "foresight by earth," and is a way to align your home harmoniously with existing sacred earth energies to improve your future. The practice originated with ancient Eastern shamans who drew mystical patterns in the sand to invoke earth energies. In medieval Europe, the famous magician and astrologer Cornelius Agrippa developed sixteen mystical symbols from these ancient shamanic patterns. Agrippa's geomancy symbols correspond to the astrological elements, the planets, and their associated crystals.

By tapping into the earth's invisible electromagnetic energy via the vibration of crystals and their associated power symbols, you can use this energy to harness what you want. Similar to the ancient Eastern principles of Feng Shui, changing the energy in your home can improve your life energy.

CONSULTING THE SYMBOLS

Simply relax and meditate on the symbols in the chart to align yourself with the earth's energies. Try to empty your mind while you run your fingers over the symbols, then choose the pattern to which you feel most connected, or that seems to "speak to you." These symbols are the silent language of the earth, representing all its different energies.

The symbol you are drawn to is the one that needs to manifest in your life right now. For example, it might be a secret desire for a new romance, an end to a difficult relationship, a high-powered career, or to move abroad. The mystical symbol you choose will reveal which goal in your life you unconsciously want to realize. By placing associated crystals in your home, you can manifest your desires.

1. VIA

Keyword: Change
Your desire: What you're really after right now is a complete change of lifestyle. You want to move on from the past and create a new future for yourself.
Crystal power: Place a piece of moonstone on your bedroom windowsill from one full moon to the next to strengthen your new cycle of growth.

2. CAUDA DRACONIS

Keyword: Completion
Your desire: You feel the need to finalize something in your life, or "wrap up" unfinished business.
Crystal power: Place a piece of obsidian in the east or south corner of your living room to cement your intention to end a relationship, be it business or personal.

3. PUER

Keyword: Passion
Your desire: You need passion in your life, be it in a sexual relationship or excitement about a new start.
Crystal power: To encourage a dynamic sex life, place a piece of fire agate or ruby under your pillow or bed.

4. FORTUNA MINOR

Keyword: Resolution
Your desire: You want to resolve a problem but you can't do this without help from others.
Crystal power: To tune into beneficial influences, place a piece of lapis lazuli in the west corner of your living room. Place a piece of jade near your front door to bring helpful influences.

5. PUELLA

Keyword: Fertility

Your desire: Puella symbolizes all things sexual, meaning that you're seeking to be more sensual, more sexually attractive.

Crystal power: Puella is associated with rose quartz. During the crescent moon, place it on your window ledge. As the moon grows, so does your fertility energy. Put the crystal under your pillow after the full moon.

6. AMISSIO

Keyword: Losing

Your desire: You want to shake off your feelings of being trapped or to untie a difficult bond.

Crystal power: To free yourself from bad relationships, place a piece of obsidian under your bed; it will strengthen your self-belief and confidence to move on.

7. CARCER

Keyword: Protection

Your desire: You're looking for stability and working with this symbol will bring spiritual and material protection.

Crystal power: To encourage a stable home life, keep a piece of black tourmaline by your main entrance door. Place a piece of onyx on your kitchen or bedroom window ledge to maximize inner strength.

8. LAETITIA

Keyword: Joy

Your desire: You want to be happier. Laetitia is shaped a bit like a rainbow and at the end of it is a pot of golden joy that will soon be yours.

Crystal power: To bring more happiness into your life, place a small selection of turquoise, aquamarine, and orange calcite in a bowl in the center of your living room table.

9. CAPUT DRACONIS

Keyword: Profit
Your desire: This symbol means "head of the dragon." You're seeking new opportunities, or want to climb the career ladder.
Crystal power: Place a piece of topaz in a drawer in the room where you do most work at home. In a west-facing corner of your living room, place azurite to give you a clear head so that you're ready to seize on money-making ventures.

10. CONJUNCTIO

Keyword: Relationship
Your desire: This symbol of marriage and partnerships reveals your search for a deep love.
Crystal power: In the southeast corner of your bedroom, place one piece of garnet to inspire romance. Placing six of these lovely red crystals wrapped in a piece of paper with the Conjunctio symbol drawn on the inside will help your soul mate to find you.

11. ACQUISITO

Keyword: Financial luck
Your desire: This symbol reveals you're desperate for something that is almost within your grasp. It will be yours very soon—particularly if associated with money.
Crystal power: In a south-facing corner of your home, place citrine for abundance and sodalite to help you make good decisions.

12. RUBEUS

Keyword: Power
Your desire: You want to rediscover your own power, by freeing yourself from manipulative people and negative emotions.
Crystal power: To liberate yourself from the power others have over you, place amethyst and shungite in the north-facing corner of your kitchen or bathroom.

13. FORTUNA MAJOR

Keyword: Success

Your desire: You're desperate for your plans to come to fruition, even if it means hard work to overcome obstacles in the way.

Crystal power: Hematite will enable you to ground your plans and blue topaz will help manifest them. Place three of each in a small pouch beside the front door to attract generosity from outside sources.

14. ALBUS

Keyword: Negotiation

Your desire: This is a time in your life when you want compromise with others.

Crystal power: For successful negotiations, in the east corner of your home, place a piece of sodalite for intuitive understanding and a piece of jasper to help you to stand up for your beliefs.

15. TRISTITIA

Keyword: Strength

Your desire: You want to remove yourself from a difficult time. You need to prioritize your own needs and feel grounded again.

Crystal power: Onyx brings order and enhances the ability to control your own destiny, no longer tied to other people's plans. Place a piece in the north-facing corner of your bedroom. Onyx is worn to defend against negativity. Black stones have protective energies and create an invisible shield around you.

16. POPULUS

Keyword: People

Your desire: You want to be adored by an audience and it's their influence that will bring you personal success.

Crystal power: In the south-facing corner of your kitchen, place rose quartz to open you up to compassionate energy and encourage good relations between you and others.

SCRYING

USING REFLECTIONS TO SEE THE FUTURE

*S*crying involves gazing at or into a shiny surface, such as a mirror or a bowl of water, to interpret patterns and see into the future. One of the most famous scryers was Elizabethan magician Dr. John Dee and his assistant Edward Kelly, who used a special black-backed mirror. At the time— the sixteenth century—mirrors were backed with tin and mercury, which didn't give such a distinct reflection. The ancient Egyptians were known to scry by staring into bowls of ink or blood, while in Persian mythology the cup of **Jamshid** contained an "elixir of immortality" in which the scryer could see the seven layers of the universe.

Pausanias, a second-century CE Greek geographer, tells of how, at the Temple of Ceres, there was a fountain. This was a place where many ill or sick people would go to discover their fate. The ill person suspended a mirror by a thread until it touched the surface of the water, having first prayed to the goddess Ceres. Then, looking in the mirror, he would see a phantom face of either Death or Health.

At the end of the nineteenth century in England and the United States, a tradition developed among young women who were looking for a husband. By gazing into a mirror in a darkened room they could see their future husband's face. A similar tradition tells of young women who walked up a flight of stairs backward, holding a candle and hand mirror. As they gazed into the mirror, they too would glimpse their future admirer.

Crystal balls became popular items for scrying. More recently, clear quartz crystals, glass objects, mirrors, and water have been used.

Seer Stones

The founder of the Latter Day Saints Movement, Joseph Smith, Jr., apparently discovered the miraculous secrets that led to the movement by scrying with the reflections of "seer stones." Smith found these stones in the 1820s, and used them to discover buried treasure. He placed the stones in the bottom of his hat, and then looked into the hat to read the miracles. Through these stones, he also translated the plates that are said to be the source of the *Book of Mormon*.

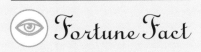

Fortune Fact

The strange word "scrying" derives from an old English word, "descry," which means "to dimly make out" or "to reveal." It comes from the same Latin root as the word "describe."

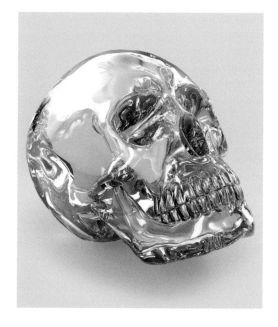

Crystal Skulls

The legendary crystal skulls of ancient Mesoamerica have been a source of mystery and controversy for decades. The handful of known skulls have defied even the most advanced scientific efforts to determine who made them, when, and most puzzling, how. In fortune-telling circles, crystal skulls are thought to be mysterious forms of computers that are able to record vibrations that occur around them. When gazing into the skull, the scryer either connects to the power of the universe, or sees all events or images of people who have been in contact with the skulls, as well as the history of the world. Many believe these skulls were carved thousands of years ago. Others think they may be relics from the legendary island of Atlantis, or proof that extraterrestrials visited the Aztecs sometime before the Spanish conquest.

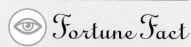 Fortune Fact

*In the Tolkien novel **The Lord of the Rings**, Galadriel, an elf ruler, invites the hero, Frodo Baggins, to look into the Mirror of Galadriel, a basin filled with water. This is where one can see visions of the past, present, and future.*

SCRYING EXERCISE

Scrying is not as immediate as using divination tools such as the Tarot or runes. You have to let your imagination work and use your intuition too. Carry out this exercise in a slightly darkened room, and whatever else, don't expect instant results. However, you will be surprised how revealing scrying can be once you get used to working with your intuition.

1. Choose either a mirror, bowl of water, or piece of white quartz crystal. Crystal balls are quite expensive and it's very difficult to "see" into them without being influenced by your own reflection. Mirrors and water are popular, but you have to look at both from an angle to avoid your own reflection. With a piece of white quartz crystal there are many nuances of light within the crystal, so it's often the easiest to use.

2. With a piece of paper and pen, sit quietly before your crystal or bowl of water, and ask yourself a simple question. It could be anything, like, "What kind of day will I have?" or "Will new romance come to me this week?"

3. Gaze at the scrying object and concentrate on your question, while you open your mind and meditate on the mirror, water, or crystal. Note down any shapes, patterns, shadows, and ripples that appear. If other ideas come into your mind as you see these shapes, make a note of these too. You can thread the ideas and the shapes together afterward. You also might see nothing but feel something, so write down your response to the session too.

INTERPRETATION OF COMMONLY SEEN SCRYING IMAGES

The interpretations given here are for some of the most popular shapes and patterns found in scrying sessions. These are not like dream interpretations, but have been traditionally associated with qualities, events, and ideas since medieval times. The symbols and meanings that follow can be used as a general guide when scrying.

Arch: A journey abroad, wedding, or new beginning.

Beetle: A difficult undertaking. A burden to carry.

Bird: Good news and great communication.

Birdcage: Obstacles, quarrels.

Bird's nest: Domestic harmony, love.

Boat: Visit from a friend, a safe refuge.

Bow and arrow: Scandal, gossip.

Branch with leaves: A birth.
Without leaves—a disappointment.

Bridge: An opportunity for success.

Building: A move of home, or change of work place.

Butterfly: Frivolity, fickleness.

Candle: Help from others, pursuit of knowledge.

Castle: Financial gain through marriage, a strong character rising to prominence.

Chair: An unexpected guest.

Clouds: Trouble ahead, but it will soon pass.

Clover: Prosperity and a sense of success.

Crab: An enemy, rival, or unwelcome visitor.

Cup: Reward for effort.

Curtain: A secret.

Dancer: Uncertainty and impulsive actions.

Deer: A dispute or quarrel.

Dog: Good friends.
If running—good news, happy meetings.

Dragon: Unforeseen changes, trouble.

Fan: Flirtation, indiscretion.

Fire: Achievement, avoid hasty overreactions.

Fist: An argument or misunderstanding.

Flower: Wish coming true.

Forked line: Decisions to be made.

Fountain: Future success and happiness.

Heart: Love and marriage, a trustworthy friend.

Horse galloping: Good news from a lover.

King: A powerful ally.

Knife: Broken relationships.

Leopard: News of a journey.

Moon: A love affair.
Crescent moon—new projects.

Mountain: Obstacle, high ambition.

Peacock: With closed tail—inertia.
With tail spread—riches, land.

Pyramid: Solid success.

Rat: Treachery, spies, and rivals.

Rose: Popularity.
Time to be loved.

Scales: A lawsuit.
Balanced scales—justice.
Unbalanced scales—injustice.

Scepter: Power, authority.

Ship: Successful journey.

Snake: Hatred, an enemy.

Star: Good health, happiness.

Sun: Happiness, success, power.

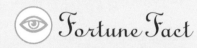

In the late nineteenth century, fraudulent mediums and similar stage acts did much to damage the reputation of real crystal ball gazing. One American mentalist, Claude Conlin—known as Alexander the Crystal Seer and Alexander, the Man Who Knows—dressed in robes and a feathered turban. He reportedly gazed into a crystal ball to read people's minds. Thought to be one of the highest-paid magic entertainment acts of the first half of the twentieth century, he lived a double life, promoting his real belief in psychic powers by writing many psychological and divination books.

Swallow: Decisiveness, unexpected journeys.

Unicorn: A secret wedding.

Wolf: Jealousy, selfishness.

Worms: Scandal, betrayal, unwanted influence.

CEROMANCY

CANDLE WAX PATTERNS AND SIGNS

*C*eromancy is the art of divining the patterns seen in melted wax. Originally it was achieved by dripping melted candle wax into a pan of cold water. It was a particular favorite method of fortune telling by Druids, Celts, and other northern cultures when candles were first used to light temples and later homes and castles. The term "ceromancy" is also now used to describe the divination of any drips or shapes formed on the side of the candle or by observing how a candle flame burns.

Try out the following exercise; just take care with dripping candle wax as it can burn.

1. Take two candles and tie them together with a ribbon.
2. Place a bowl of cold water on the table or floor, and then hold the candles at an angle so that the wax will drip directly onto the water. Now light them and let the wax slowly drip into the bowl.
3. Interpret any shapes formed by the hot wax as it solidifies. Some traditional interpretations of the shapes are listed on p. 178, but it is also your own intuitive interpretations depending on your current situation that will really count.
4. You can also just light one shorter candle in a candle holder and watch the drips falling down the side while you meditate on the candle flame about what you want for your future. Once the drips have built up into a mass down the sides or in the holder, you can begin to interpret the patterns or shapes you see.

BEHIND THE SIGNS

Druid Fortune Telling

In Greek mythology, the Dryades were oak nymphs associated with the priestesses of Artemis. In pre-patriarchal Europe, the cult of Artemis was a mystery religion exclusive to women, who practiced rites in oak or hazel groves in northwestern Europe. Later, in Celtic Europe, this developed into a cult of bardic soothsayers or seers, known as Druids. It was believed that Druids were consulted by Irish kings and legendary heroes. Medb, the Queen of Connacht, consulted her personal Druid before setting off to war. When he saw in the wax patterns the shape of a helmet, indicating danger, Medb delayed the battle for several weeks until an auspicious omen such as a round table appeared in the wax. Dalgn, the personal Druid of Eochu Airem, the high king of Ireland around 100 BCE, used candle wax to find the king's wife, Etain, who had run away with Midir.

INTERPRETATIONS OF VARIOUS PATTERNS

Airplane: A trip.

Anchor: Your loved one is true.

Ball: Your problem will not last very long.

Beans: Money difficulties.

Bed: A vacation would be good for you.

Bells: A wedding.

Bridge: Take a chance.

Broom: Make a change.

Candle: Spiritual growth.

Chain: Go ahead with your plans.

Circle: Reconciliation.

Cloud: Something or someone threatens you.

Dog: Your self-esteem is too low.

Ear: Be alert for an opportunity to advance in your work.

Egg: New developments soon.

Fan: A surprise is in store for you.

Feather: The problem will be solved.

Fish: Someone will betray you.

Ghost: Someone from the past is looking for you.

Grass: Good fortune is approaching.

Hat: A change of location is indicated.

Heart: A friendship will turn into love.

House: Better times are coming.

Key: A setback in plans should be expected.

Ladder: Take steps to change your attitude toward an old friend.

Pen: Expect a letter from a relative.

Pipe: Peace and comfort.

Ring: Marriage may be possible.

Scissors: Separation.

Shoe: Be suspicious of a new acquaintance.

Snake: Be on guard against an enemy.

Spiderweb: Pleasant happenings.

Star: Happiness.

Sun: Good fortune.

Table: An abundance of blessings.

Umbrella: Trouble is coming.

Walking stick: Get out of the house and visit friends.

Wheel: One who has been away will return soon.

Witch: Danger will pass you by.

CANDLE POWER

The ancient Egyptians were the first to use candles with wicks around 3000 BCE by dipping rolled papyrus repeatedly in melted animal fat or beeswax. The resulting candles were used to light their homes, to aid travelers at night, and in religious ceremonies. Many other early civilizations developed candles with wicks using waxes made from available plants and insects.

Early Chinese candles are said to have been molded in paper tubes, using rolled rice paper for the wick, and wax from an indigenous insect that was combined with seeds. In Japan, candles were made of wax extracted from tree nuts, while in India, candle wax was made by boiling the fruit of the cinnamon tree.

Most early Western cultures relied primarily on candles rendered from animal fat known as tallow. However, the smell of tallow was particularly unpleasant, so during the Middle Ages beeswax candles were introduced in Europe. Unlike animal-based tallow, beeswax burned purely and cleanly, without producing a smoky flame. It also emitted a pleasant sweet smell rather than the foul odor of tallow. By the thirteenth century, candle-making had become a guild craft in England and France. Candle-makers, known as chandlers, made candles for each village house from the family's carefully stored kitchen fats. With the demand for candles increasing, by the end of the fourteenth century candle shops were big business.

GLOSSARY

Arcana/Arcanum: The two distinctly different series of cards in a tarot deck are the Major and Minor Arcana. "*Arcanum*" is the Latin for "secret." Its plural form is "*arcana*," so the Major and Minor Arcana are "big secrets" and "little secrets."

Archetype: Universal force, quality, or pattern of behavior that operates autonomously in the depths of the human psyche.

Astrology: An ancient system of divination that studies the patterns and placement of the planets as they appear to travel through the zodiac belt.

Chakra: Sanskrit word meaning "wheel," which is an energy center of the subtle body.

Ch'i: Chinese term for the universal energy that flows through everything.

Collective consciousness: Another term for the cosmic storehouse of all knowledge.

Crystal ball: A ball usually made of clear quartz crystal, used for divination purposes.

Dowsing: A means of divination using pendulums or rods. Also used to find missing objects, water, or even people.

Elements: In Western astrology there are four elements—Fire, Earth, Air, and Water—that represent qualities and characteristics in people. In Chinese astrology there are five elements—Fire, Earth, Water, Wood, and Metal—that also correspond to various qualities and personalities.

Freemason: A member of an international order of fellowship, criticized for their secrecy and supposed occult rites and practices. The original freemasons were fourteenth-century skilled stonemasons who used secret signs to communicate.

Numerology: The art of divination using numbers considered to be the core of everything in the universe. The primary numbers, 1 to 9, vibrate to different frequencies and these vibrations echo through the universe.

Occult: From a Latin word "*occultus*," meaning "hidden," or "mysterious." Used from the fifteenth century as a verb meaning "to conceal." It was favored in the nineteenth century to describe supernatural and magical beliefs and practices.

Oracle: A place, object, or person through whom a deity or spiritual force is believed to speak and reveal hidden knowledge.

Order of the Golden Dawn: An influential occultist group founded in 1888 by Willian Wynn Wescott, a master freemason, and his flamboyant friend, Samuel Mathers. Drawing on many esoteric beliefs, Mathers fused Egyptian magical systems with medieval magic texts as well as eastern esoteric beliefs to create a workable magic system.

Pentacles: Magical, disk-shaped objects used as a symbol in Tarot for the element of Earth. Often referred to as "coins" or "disks." The word derives from a Latin word, "*pentaculum*," relating to the pentagram, or five-pointed mystical star.

Psyche: The Greek word for soul. In contemporary psychology, it is equated with the mind.

Scrying: A divination technique using the surface of reflective water, a mirror, or crystal to view and interpret shapes and patterns.

Sixth sense: Also known as ESP and intuition, the sixth sense is our ability to contact otherworldly or spiritual realms through means other than the usual five senses.

Storehouse of all Knowledge: Also known as the Akashic Library, this is a storehouse that exists beyond time and space and contains information of everything that has happened, and that will happen, in the universe.

Sybil: A prophetess and seer, usually from ancient Greece.

Symbol: A manifest sign of something occult, mystical, or hidden. Rooted in the Greek word *"symbolon,"* meaning "something thrown together."

Synchronicity: A meaningful coincidence or set of events that share the same symbolic features and give personal meaning to an individual. It is also the belief that everything in the universe is interconnected, and that events and patterns in the tea cup, Tarot, or in someone's life and anywhere on Earth are all an interface of an invisible force. The randomness of divination is itself part of this process.

Yin and Yang: The two energies that make up the "ch'i," or the universal energy that flows through everything. Yin is the feminine, receptive energy, and Yang the masculine, dynamic energy.

BIBLIOGRAPHY

Bartlett, Sarah.
The Tarot Bible.
London, UK: Octopus/Godsfield, 2006.

Blum, Ralph.
The Book of Runes.
London, UK: Connections Book Publishing, 2000.

Butler, Gail.
Crystal and Gemstone Divination.
Upland, CA: Gem Guides, 2008.

Carter, Hilary H.
Numerology Made Easy.
London, UK: Dodona Books, 2012.

"Cheiro."
Cheiro's Numerology and Astrology:
The Book of Fate and Fortune.
London, UK: Orient Paperbacks, 2005.

Fairchild, Dennis.
The Fortune-telling Handbook: The Interactive Guide
to Tarot, Palm Reading and More.
Philadelphia, PA: Running Press, 2003.

Gerrard, Katie.
Odin's Gateways.
London, UK: Avalonia, 2009.

Goodwin, Matthew Oliver.
Numerology: The Complete Guide.
Pompton Plains, NJ: New Page Books, 2005.

Greer, John Michael.
The Art and Practice of Geomancy: Divination,
Magic, and Earth Wisdom of the Renaissance.
Newburyport, MA: Weiser Books, 2009.

Greer, Mary K.
Tarot for Yourself: A Workbook for Personal
Transformation.
Pompton Plains, NJ: New Page Books, 2002.

Hall, Judy.
The Crystal Bible.
London, UK: Godsfield Press, 2009.

Hawk, Ambrose.
Exploring Scrying: How to Divine the Future and
Make the Most of It.
Pompton Plains, NJ: New Page Books, 2009.

Jung, C. G.
I Ching or Book of Changes.
London, UK: Arkana, 1989.

Kemp, Gillian.
The Fortune Telling Book: Reading Crystal Balls,
Tea Leaves, Playing Cards, and Everyday Omens of
Love and Luck.
London, UK: Orion, 2001.

Nichols, Sallie.
Jung and Tarot: An Archetypal Journey.
Newburyport, MA: Weiser Books, 1980.

Peschel, Lisa.
A Practical Guide to the Runes: Their Uses in
Divination and Magick.
Woodbury, MN: Llewellyn, 1989.

Secter, Mondo.
The I Ching Handbook: Decision-Making With and
Without Divination.
Berkeley, CA: North Atlantic Books, 2002.

Valverde, Laeticia.
The Palmistry Workbook: A Step-by-step Guide to
the Art of Palm Reading.
London, UK: Apple Press, 2006.

Walker, Barbara.
The Woman's Encyclopedia of Myths and Secrets.
London, UK: HarperCollins, 1983.

Willis, Tony.
The Runic Workbook: Understanding and Using the
Power of Runes.
Dartford, UK: Aquarian Press, 1986.

Wilson, Joyce.
The Complete Book of Palmistry.
London, UK: Bantam Doubleday Del, 1988.

ACKNOWLEDGMENTS

*M*any thanks to everyone at Quid, especially James and Lucy, for all their help and good work. Also, not forgetting my agent, Chelsey Fox, for her never-ending support, and my family for being who they are.

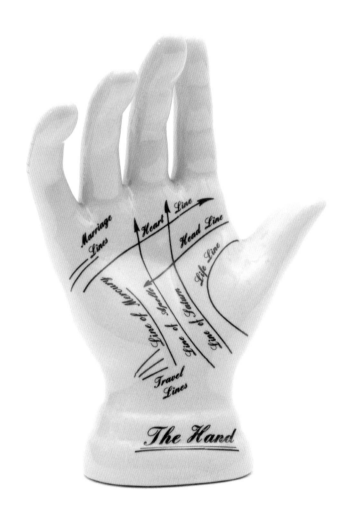

PICTURE CREDITS

138 © Michaela Stejskalova | Shutterstock
139 © Photosani | Shutterstock
140 © Martin Novak | Shutterstock
141 and 146 Orange carnelian
   © Sergey Lavrentev | Shutterstock
141 and 146, 148 Tourmaline
   © Imfoto | Shutterstock
141 and 146 Blue lace agate
   © MarcelClemens | Shutterstock
141 and 146, 169 Onyx
   © Fernando Sanchez Cortes | Shutterstock
141 and 146, 148 Lapis lazuli
   © Only Fabrizio | Shutterstock
141 and 146, 149 Red agate
   © Howard Sandler | Shutterstock
141 and 145, 149, 169 Topaz
   © TinaImages | Shutterstock
141 and 145 Opal
   © Alexander Hoffmann | Shutterstock
141 and 145, 174 Clear quartz
   © Fribus Ekaterina | Shutterstock
142 and 144, 149 Red carnelian © Fernando
   Sanchez Cortes | Shutterstock
142 and 144, 167, 169 Rose quartz © optimarc |
   Shutterstock
142 and 144 Citrine © Ilizia | Shutterstock
142 and 144 Tiger's eye
   © Sergey Lavrentev | Shutterstock
142 and 144 Peridot © Nastya22 | Shutterstock
142 and 144, 149 Jade
   © Alexander Hoffmann | Shutterstock
142 and 145, 148 Malachite
   © Zelenskaya | Shutterstock
142 and 145, 148, 167 Turquoise
   © Alexander Hoffmann | Shutterstock
142 and 145, 166, 167 Obsidian
   © Siim Sepp | Shutterstock
142 and 145 Amber © MaraZe | Shutterstock
143 © Martin Novak | Shutterstock
147 © Diego Cervo | Shutterstock

148 © Deklofenak | Shutterstock
150 © Donatella Tandelli | Shutterstock
153 © Monika Wisniewska | Shutterstock
154 © Gilles Paire | Shutterstock
157 © Anneka | Shutterstock
158 © M. Unal Ozmen | Shutterstock
160 © Elle1 | Shutterstock
164 © ArtFamily | Shutterstock
165 © Mark III Photonics | Shutterstock
166 Ruby © Imfoto | Shutterstock
   Jadite © Sergey Lavrentev | Shutterstock
168 Azurite © joyfuldesigns | Shutterstock
   Red garnet © Imfoto | Shutterstock
   Citrine © Ilizia | Shutterstock
169 Sodalite © Martina Osmy | Shutterstock
170 © Ilya Shapovalov | Shutterstock
172 © | Shutterstock
173 © Subbotina Anna | Shutterstock
175 Public domain
176 © Aksenova Natalya | Shutterstock
177 © Serov | Shutterstock
179 © RiceWithSugar | Shutterstock
181 © Michaela Stejskalova | Shutterstock
182 © bluesnote | Shutterstock
184 © AMC Photography | Shutterstock
185 © Tony Moran | Shutterstock
191 © Martina Vaculikova | Shutterstock
192 © mama_mia | Shutterstock

24, 28, 31–42, 45–55, 58–59, 61–64 Universal Tarot
   © Lo Scarabeo s.r.l. All rights reserved.

Behind the Signs recurring image
   © Photosani | Shutterstock

INDEX